MOR. HILL OCT 31 '81

y916.4 Daly, Maureen.
D15 Moroccan roundabout.

300

530363

Santa Clara County Free Library

MOROCCAN ROUNDABOUT

Books by Maureen Daly

SEVENTEENTH SUMMER

SMARTER AND SMOOTHER

MY FAVORITE STORIES

THE PERFECT HOSTESS

WHAT'S YOUR P.Q.?

TWELVE AROUND THE WORLD

PATRICK VISITS THE FARM

PATRICK TAKES A TRIP

SPANISH ROUNDABOUT

SIXTEEN AND OTHER STORIES

MOROCCAN ROUNDABOUT

With William P. McGivern

MENTION MY NAME IN MOMBASA

MOROCCAN ROUNDABOUT

by Maureen Daly

ILLUSTRATED WITH PHOTOGRAPHS

Dodd, Mead & Company

NEW YORK - 1961

Copyright © 1961 by Maureen Daly

All rights reserved

No part of this book may be reproduced in any form without permission in writing from the publisher

"Teen-Ager Moroccan Style" reprinted by permission of the *American Girl,* a magazine for all girls published by the Girl Scouts of the U.S.A.

Library of Congress Catalog Card Number: 61-10361

Printed in the United States of America

by The Haddon Craftsmen, Inc., Scranton, Penna.

y914.6
D15

.... for Ahmed and Doris Kaye because
"it's good for Milton"

Our warmest thanks to Mr. Phineas Toby of the Moroccan Chamber of Commerce and to the Information Division of the French Embassy for furnishing us with pictures for this book. Through their kindness, we are able to show others some glimpses of the magnificent and most interesting country of Morocco.

Contents

Illustrations

Photographic supplement follows page 84

Since the fabled days of the Barbary pirates, Morocco's long coast lines have furnished good ports for commercial and fishing vessels. Ships of all nations pick up outgoing cargoes of Moroccan minerals, citrus fruits, cereals and cork. White domed building in foreground is saint's shrine.

Goats forage for fruit of argan tree; fruit pits are squeezed for lamp oil.

Chief mountain range is the Atlas, with many peaks perpetually snow-capped.

Tiznit is an oasis town, surrounded by high brown walls and built around a sacred pool. Jewelry-manufacturing center for the south, it is an active, commercial area, served by both rickety buses and camel traffic. Mosque in background shows protruding poles, built for dead souls to "roost."

The brilliance of orange trees against red clay walls, the fragrance of jasmine and lilies, the distant shine of snow on blue mountains —this is Marrakesh. A garden city fed by mountain rivers, it is the center of "Red Morocco." Visitors from all the world seek out this beauty spot.

Each dusk, the cooling air smells of hot-fat doughnuts, donkeys and fresh melons. Storytellers chant out ancient tales; dancers and musicians perform before applauding circles; snake charmers thrill the crowd with fang-mouthed serpents. This is Djema-Fna-Place, the market heart of Marrakesh.

Moroccans are skilled handicraftsmen. Behind such doors are homes with carved ceilings, intricately tiled floors and lanterns cut to give patterned light; beauty behind high walls, huddled close on narrow streets.

Delicate handicraft work marks Moroccan architecture. This palace shows arches with spun-sugar workmanship, in courtyard designed to enhance both sunlight and shadow. But only the very wealthy enjoy such home beauties.

In this land of contrasts, modern cities such as Port Lyautey are never far from primitive country villages. Most big towns are distinctly divided between the Moroccan-planned *medinas* and the wide-street, skyscraper towns built by the French, "little Parises" set down on foreign soil.

A Moroccan garden must have three things: running water, cool shadows and flower scents. Most city homes are built around open courtyard, planted as garden, used as sitting room, play area or sunny spot to dry family wash.

Annual Feast of the Sheep is a day of prayer and rejoicing. Here crowd waits before mosque for word that the sacrificial mutton has met "blessed death."

Every Friday, the Moslem holy day, the King rides ceremoniously to near-by mosque for noon-time prayers. In each major town, King's representatives, splendidly garbed and escorted, make similar trips to offer prayers to Allah.

Chapter I

MOROCCO—WHO, WHAT, WHERE?

In history, Morocco is very old and very young. Centuries ago, Roman legions marched across its plains; crumbling stone ruins still mark the history they etched upon this land. In its *old* history, Morocco knew conquests from northern Europe and Arabia; later came the Spanish and the Portuguese. Some pages of its past record are almost blank, blacked-out by the isolation and destruction of bitter internal wars.

But today Morocco is open to the world in a bright new phase of life. It was reborn in independence in 1956, when the flourish of a French pen—after forty-four years of domination—gave this country status as an independent and sovereign state.

Whether it waves from on top the King's royal palace in Rabat or flutters from a straw-thatched farmer's hut in the *bled,* the red and green flag of Morocco now flies in new hope and freedom.

««««««««« »»»»»»»»»

The Arabic name for Morocco is *El Maghreb el Aksa*—meaning "the farthest west." And it is the farthest west of all the Arabic-speaking countries, lapped on its western shores by the long waves of the Atlantic Ocean. Its northern boundaries look out on the blue of the Mediterranean and its eastern and southern borders merge into the soil of neighboring Algeria. Perched as it is on the humped left shoulder of Africa, this country seems about to be shrugged into the sea by the great mother continent.

Morocco is a country of rare scenic beauty, with mountain ranges reminiscent of Colorado, farm lands rolled out flat as Kansas and brilliant sun and bright flowers similar to those of Mexico and California. It has been said that Morocco is a "hot country with a cold climate." The weather ranges from arid heat in summer to brief, bitter winters, when coastal areas are lashed with winds and freezing rains and the mountains can become impassable with snow.

It is a country in many ways blessed, though all the blessings have not yet been "developed." Farm lands are fertile, mountains abound with minerals and the seas are rich with fish. Yet a man may warm his shoulders in the sun and trek along country roads bright with daisies and poppies—and still toil uncounted hours to maintain his family minimally on a scant $175 average income per year.

«««««««« »»»»»»»»

The population of this country is about 10,000,000 and Moroccans are characteristically capable, quick-witted and tenacious. They have long been known for two marked but contrasting qualities—fierceness in a fight and warm hospitality.

Most Moroccans are light-skinned people, though centuries of infiltration from lower Africa has introduced Negroid strains. These darker Moroccans are as much a part of the country and its privileges as their fairer national brothers.

Women above the teen years cultivate plumpness as a female attraction, but otherwise the people are chiefly slim and agile, with sharp features and alert carriage. At his most attractive, the male Moroccan has some of the most pleasing physical qualities of the Spanish and Italians—smooth skin, bright dark eyes and thick, lustrous hair.

These are an energetic, vital people; not too interested perhaps in joining and aping the ways of the western world, but much alive within their own country and their own culture.

«««««««« »»»»»»»»

Moroccans may be called a number of things: Arabs, Berbers, Rifs, etc., and all would be correct because the country is made up of several racial stocks, united as Moroccans. The two principal stocks are Berber and Arab, with the former predominating. Today, as a general thing, Berbers live in the country and farm the land, Arabs live in the cities and are in trade.

Berbers are believed to have migrated from different parts of Europe into Morocco sometime during the dim ages. An Egyptian inscription, dated 1700 B.C., refers to "Berbers" living in North Africa. Some say the word "berber" is a corruption of "barbarian" because early traders and seafarers, touching Moroccan shores by boat, found the fierce, light-skinned inhabitants just that—barbaric.

Early centuries invasions from Arabia brought the first Arabs to Morocco. With them came their language and customs. They stayed to intermarry and become the Moroccans they are today.

The official language in present-day Morocco is Arabic but most Berbers still commonly speak their own language, sometimes almost barring themselves from communication with other Moroccans by favoring obscure tribal dialects. Because of the long years in which French and Spanish controlled and did business in Morocco, most sophisticated Moroccans can speak both these languages. In fact, in the *souks* or market places of northern Morocco it is not Arabic *or* Berber but Spanish that is used as the common language.

«««««««« »»»»»»»»

In land-mass, Morocco has a total area of 190,000 square miles or about twice the size of Minnesota. Much of this land is dominated by mountains, the chief range of which is called the Atlas Mountains. This great range, extending from the Atlantic Ocean on into Algeria, varies in elevation from 5,000 to 13,000 feet. Many of the peaks are perpetually capped with snow, giving the valleys below a much-needed water supply and helping to cool the air in the heat of summer. South of the Atlas range, except for occasional natural (and now artificial) oases, the land turns desert, anticipating the sand-ribbed wastes of the Great Sahara.

To a small-farm, agriculture country such as Morocco, water is a constant essential and worry. The rainy winter is short; rains are usually brief, violent and unpredictable. Some years, the fear of drought is the darkest cloud hanging over the dry farm lands. For centuries, the Arab farmer has tried to nurture his fields with careful though primitive irrigation. In the last forty-four years, French engineers planned and built a number of highly efficient reservoirs and irrigation systems. The work is still far from completed but, with proper water conservation and distribution, vast now-dry acres may become fertile and bloom rewardingly.

«««««««« »»»»»»»»

Whether they drive French-financed tractors or follow their own donkeys behind hand-guided plows, eighty-five per cent of all Moroccans make their living through farming, many cultivating just a few acres.

Cereals are the most important crop. Then come fruit, citrus and sweet, green vegetables, olives, cork, almonds, wine (for export) and livestock. Only about three per cent of the farmers use modern farming methods and the crops are plagued by drought and the frequent onslaughts of locusts; hence the current output is far below what it someday may be.

Mining is the next most important industry in this nation. Most of the mineral wealth is still unexploited, and the development of mining has slowed down considerably since the country gained independence and took over much of an industry with which the Moroccans had little experience and for which they could provide too-few trained workers.

About seventeen per cent of the total world output of phosphate comes from Morocco, and its unmined reserves are considered among the largest in the world. Other important and available minerals are iron ore, lead, zinc, manganese, cobalt and that "black gold," anthracite coal. Morocco is considered to have the largest anthracite deposit in the whole Mediterranean area, still mostly untouched.

There *is* oil in Morocco. Some has been discovered. A small quantity is produced and refined there today. Nationalist Moroccans are convinced that their land will eventually become one of the richest oil-producing countries on earth. Their hopes are buttressed by the constant interest of other nations who are quite willing to contribute capital and "experimental teams" to search the oil out.

«««««««« »»»»»»»»

There is little heavy industry in this country and eighty-five per cent of what exists is concentrated in the great port city of Casablanca. But it *is* a nation of skilled, artistic small craftsmen. A visit to the workshops of any *souk,* with a master and a few young apprentices at work with the most primitive tools, would make one suspect that the Industrial Revolution had never happened at all.

Moroccans are specialists in leather and metal work, weaving and inlay crafts. With leather, often worked over until it is as supple as satin, they make saddles, bags, wallets, book covers, ottomans and slippers. Many of these are wonderfully dyed and stamped with gold patterns. Metal work includes trays, teapots, candlesticks, lanterns, etc., made in materials varying from iron to glistening brass, shaped and etched magnificently. Weaving includes colorful robes and rugs, as well as the tightly woven wool fabric used for the Moroccan garments, *djellabas* and *burnooses.* Most of the inlay work is done on chests, small tables for supporting trays or tiny, cabinets with many drawers, used to hold jewelry. The inlay is most commonly mother-of-pearl, though some excellent designs are made by patiently pounding strands of gold wire into soft woods.

Most of the handwork is done by a master craftsman, assisted by teen-aged boys who are willing to labor for next to nothing to learn a trade. There is little regulation of working hours or conditions; work may start with sunrise, end with sundown. In winter, apprentices may crouch on cold stone floors; in summer, the only breeze and light may come through a single open door. But the finished products are impressive and, in keeping with their sensual appreciations ("Allah desires your ease"), Moroccans greatly enjoy the skills of their craftsmen.

About three million dollars a year in leather goods is exported to world markets from Morocco, but most of the craftwork is sold within the nation itself.

«««««««« »»»»»»»»

Today, about seventy-five per cent of the people in this colorful country are still illiterate. Millions who can chant out from memory the exquisite verses of the Koran could not read the headlines of the daily newspaper. Many Moroccans feel this is just as it should be; a man does not need to read or write to earn a living and please his God. But the new government is determined that Morocco *will* become literate—and is new educating native specialists who can lead and develop the business and industry of their own country with success.

When the Moroccans became independent in 1956, the educational roster stood thus: out of the total population there were only five graduate professors, one polytechnician, one doctor of law, three public works engineers, eighteen lawyers, forty-two agricultural engineers, twenty-one medical doctors, forty-two professors of Arabic—and less than one hundred university graduates.

Literate Moroccans are today bitter and vocal about what caused this serious lack of "education in depth." When the French Protectorate took over in 1912, it is explained, Morocco—like most Arab countries prior to that date—had an educational system limited to small private, religious schools called *Kittab,* Koran schools, where male children went for two or three years, to learn, memorize and recite the Holy Book, the Koran. A very few went on to higher schools, where they had the opportunity to learn to read and write Arabic and a little arithmetic; but these higher schools *(medersas)* were also chiefly concerned with religion rather than a broader training and education.

Under the Protectorate, the French promptly organized schools taught in French, with French teachers and a curriculum identical to that offered in France. Naturally, say Moroccans today, we did not want our children to go to schools where no Arabic was taught. A few Moroccan students did apply, but were turned down, Moroccans insist. Near the end of its Protectorate, the French did maintain a few schools where some Arabic was taught—but it was "too little, too late." In 1956, when the French withdrew from the country, only about one in eight Moroccan children had had any schooling *at all.*

«««««««« »»»»»»»»

Today, about thirty-five per cent of all primary age children are in school, of one type or another. French-built institutions are crammed to accomodate classes ranging from 50 to 18—the average with 70 pupils per class. "Freedom to attend school" was announced to the whole country with the issuance of 3,000,000 pamphlets on education. The response was overwhelming—and temporarily very inconvenient.

Much of the teaching is now done in Arabic, though often by former religious students who can read and write but have had little training in the subjects they teach. An attempt was made to train "volunteer teachers" in remote areas by radio instructions. However, not enough readers-and-writers could be found to make this venture successful.

Nevertheless, the approach to the need for education and the handicaps to be overcome is most realistic. When it was discovered that it was not possible to teach elementary science and mathematics in Arabic (no qualified teachers, no textbooks), it was decided that those subjects would be taught in French "until further notice." Former King Mohammed V introduced the idea of "adult education" for older Arabs with night-time classes in primary schools. In a much publicized session, he taught the first class in reading for men himself, while his daughter, H.R.H. Princess Lalla Aisha, taught the women.

The Ministry of Education makes frequent radio broadcasts, urging young people to get into schools, to study and work hard to become educated citizens. These programs have become very popular. I remember listening to a broadcast in a little tailor's workshop last summer. The apprentices listened seriously and then roared with laughter. The speaker was spicing up his advice with jokes about the "troubles of the stupid," and his audience loved it.

It will take decades to organize a sound educational system in this country—and more decades to make that system effective, especially in the rural and mountain areas. But Morocco has come alive to her own needs. Many of her people are already proud—proud of the hopes, proud of the plans and proud of what is to come. . . .

Just this summer, having heard much about the ambitious educational building program, I asked a very intelligent guide in Tangier to show me one of the new schools. He said he would. That afternoon, we drove out of the city on a long, hilly road, leading upward through fertile farm fields and passing several little country villages. We stopped finally on a grassy, wind-swept hill, looking down steeply to the crashing Atlantic. Out of the car, we stood in the wind, looking over the ocean, the fields behind and some distant mountains.

"But where is the school?" I asked.

The guide pointed back to the suburbs of Tangier, then to

a spot on the mountains and then down to his own feet. "They will be there—there—and here," he said proudly.

But the grass on which we stood was still peacefully growing with tiny blue iris and a flock of black goats grazed nearby, undisturbed by the sound of school bells or the rush of scholars' feet.

«««««««« »»»»»»»»

It is almost impossible to get a calm answer from either a Moroccan or a Frenchman, on why the French Protectorate came to an end. An irate Frenchman will likely shout (as I was shouted at), "They are a backward people—stupid. They want nothing but to sleep in the sun. Now that we are gone, the grass will grow in the streets of Casablanca."

A bitter Arab would say, "It was *everything, everything* for the French. We made France rich while our people worked as slaves in our own country."

Of course, neither statement comes quite near the truth. France and Morocco made a political union in the early twentieth century, when many such unions were being made. They dissolved that union, after bitterness and bloodshed, at a time in history when such unions were being dissolved. . . .

«««««««« »»»»»»»»

The time was ripe for empire-grabbing. In 1904, Great Britain officially recognized Morocco as "within the French sphere of influence." France then gave England similar recognition in regard to Egypt. That same year, France granted Spain a "special interest" in Morocco and, at a conference held in Algeciras, in southern Spain, France and Spain together were granted privilege in policing Morocco.

Morocco, at this time, was torn and weakened by internal

wars between rival tribes. Sometimes the Sultan called in Spanish soldiers to quell uprisings, sometime French. Now the Germans became uneasy, fearful that they might be left out of sharing the colonial spoils of Africa. In a fit of political pique, they sent a gunboat to the Moroccan port of Agadir, to ride ominously just off shore. A French-German conference resulted. The Germans agreed to a hands-off policy in Morocco, in return for a piece of the French Congo.

In 1912, Sultan Moulay Hafid of Fez called on the French once more for military assistance. Uprisings in the Sultans's territory had gotten out of control. The French responded with troops and, shortly afterward, the French and several Moroccan representatives agreed to a "French Protectorate" of the whole country. Independently, France signed a second agreement, assigning a portion of northern Morocco to Spain. The arrangement lasted for forty-four years.

«««««««« »»»»»»»»

Today, about 380,000 Frenchmen still live and work in Morocco; another 35,000 went back to their homeland after 1956. Many of the resident French have lived there for three generations and their children speak Arabic and Berber, as well as they do their own language. For nearly half a century, immense French capital, energy and know-how were poured into this country, and some of the best Morocco vineyards, dairies and farms were French-planned and French owned. The French contributions to the country as a whole were many. They built roads, hotels and factories; they introduced advanced irrigation systems, mining methods, developed efficient port facilities. Through French-staffed hospitals and mobile units, they did much to educate Moroccans in disease prevention and child care. The national death rate went down; tuberculosis became somewhat less of a menace; the eye diseases which plague Morocco decreased.

In 1945, after World War II, the government of France announced that it was going to make Morocco "the showcase of the abilities and glories of France." But for all France wanted to *give* to this nation, Morocco felt the "take" was too much. This country was tired of foreign rule—and foreign profits in foreign banks. The spirit of freedom was in the air all around the earth, and Morocco was determined to fly her own flag and control her own destinies.

In a following chapter we discuss the now-deceased King Mohammed V, the ruler who led his people to ultimate freedom in March, 1956. Self-rule has brought with it special problems. Without the impetus of complete control, many French businessmen lost interest in the "showcase" country. Factories were closed, capital was withdrawn—and staggering unemployment and resultant poverty swept the country.

Today, there are over one million unemployed in Morocco —and the figure is likely to grow. Morocco is floundering about, looking for new investors and new markets. Trade agreements have been signed with Russia, Communist China, and East and West Germany. France is still much in evidence in Morocco, however. This new country—which felt it could not live with France within her borders—now finds life hard without her.

But, as the government tells its people often, survival needs courage. And the Moroccans have never been short on courage.

«««««««« »»»»»»»»

The United States and this Arab state have been on friendly terms for a long, long time. A treaty of friendship was first signed way back in 1787. At that time, George Washington wrote the Sultan of Morocco:

"The encouragement which your Majesty has been pleased generously to give our commerce with your dominions; the punctuality with which you have caused the Treaty with us to be observed; and the just and generous measures taken in the name of Captain Proctor (one of the U.S. treaty negotiators) make a deep impression on the United States and confirm their respect for, and attachment to, your Imperial Majesty. It gives me great pleasure to have this opportunity of assuring your Majesty that, while I remain at the head of this Nation, I shall not cease to promote every measure that may conduce to the friendship and harmony which so happily subsist between your Empire and them. . . ."

Since that note was written, we have maintained cordial diplomatic relations with Morocco, even through the period of the French Protectorate. However, Morocco today does not look on the United States totally without criticism. In 1950 and 1951, in agreements signed solely with the French, the United States arranged for—and subsequently built—five huge airbases on Moroccan soil. Thousands of Americans have trained here and many American families are in residence at the base. North Africa's perfect flying weather and its strategic location make the bases extremely important to us.

But all negotiations were made with French authorities. It is little wonder that, once back in power, the head of the government of Morocco exercised his newly-reeestablished rights as head of state—and informed the United States government that the bases were not welcome. Dignity had been offended; dignity had been avenged. Discussions still continue —and the exact date of withdrawal of these military installations has not been decided.

«««««««« »»»»»»»»

All this is part of the "big history" of Morocco, the kind of fact and statistic that makes the front pages of newspapers and the back pages of textbooks. But to understand and appreciate a remote and strange country such as Morocco, it is more necessary to look at the "little histories," the way of life of the people, the individual dramas that make a nation. And it is to a close-up view of this "land farthest west" that we devote the following chapters of this book.

Chapter II

KING MOULAY HASSAN II—AND FRIENDS

AT A QUICK glance, Morocco is a nation of look-alike people. The tiny veiled and white-swathed figure pushing through the market crowds is just another young girl—until, perhaps, you see her eyes. Or the tall, brown-skinned guide in Marrakesh, erect in white *djellaba* and red *fez,* is just another Arab—until he tells you his story. The ragged shepherd on one hilltop is just like the ragged shepherd on another hilltop—until you have watched both for a while. The concealment brought about by the uniform clothing and the concealment of the *casbah* way of life *may* make one man seem exactly like another—and even interchangeable with another—until, suddenly, some individuality reveals itself. Then each Moroccan, like each other human being, is a little different. And each adds his own indispensable bit of color and characterization to the motley Moroccan landscape. Each is remembered for something special. . . .

Ahmed Mohammed Boonan, for instance, stays in one's memory because he wanted so much to be *liked.* We saw him first in the central square of Tetuan, a busy, Spanish-influenced town in the north country. He smiled at us by way of introduction, the bright sunlight glinting on his two solid gold front teeth. He was impeccably groomed, with a spotless white Western-type shirt showing above his *djellaba* and when he came to our table, at a sidewalk café, the air was scented with a smell like dusty lilacs.

Ahmed was a guide, at our service if we wanted him, he explained, pulling a sheaf of letters from an inside pocket, letters from "friends" he had guided in the past. He spoke five languages—Arabic, Spanish, French, English—and a little German, but could read only Arabic. From the pack of letters, he pulled out one written by the head of the Bartenders' Union of New York City. "Read," he said. In his confidence, Ahmed knew the letter was a friendly one. In it, the man thanked him for his kindness during a trip to Tetuan the previous summer and urged him to "look me up if you're ever in New York."

Ahmed became our guide for the next few days, working as earnestly as if the future of all Morocco depended on his salesmanship. On foot, we toured the rugged streets of the casbah, stopping at every third or fourth shop to be introduced to an acquaintance of Ahmed's. He had been born and raised here and knew every café and back alley as a farm boy might know every rock and tree in the surrounding fields.

Ahmed was twenty-two, exceedingly handsome, chiefly because of his energy and expressive eyes. And he created a humorous intimacy by staring us full in the face every half hour or so to ask, in an almost pleading voice, "You *like* what I show you?"

The curiosity of his personality began to demonstrate itself the second day. Though he worked part-time as a guide for a living, he refused to take any fee after the day of our first meeting. His explanation: first he had been a *guide,* now he was a *friend.* No protests would change his mind. He even apologized about not being able to afford to pick up the checks for meals shared, though he insisted on paying his share right down to the last franc.

Above all, Ahmed was amusing. He loved to laugh and always laughed again if he found he had made us smile. One day, we hired a car to drive over the twisting roads between Tetuan and Tangier. On one curved peak, where the valleys were so deep that the shrubs showed blue at the bottom, the car stalled. The driver got out to put his head under the hood and we stood on the roadside, feeling the hot breezes blowing over us like warm steam. Nearby, a group of Moroccan road workers, equipped with nothing more than short pickaxes, straw baskets and their bare hands, were hacking at the roadbed. In curiosity, they drew near us, looking—with their ragged turbans, beards and perspiration-stained faces—like a group of Biblical bandits. Ahmed asked their names and then made introductions all around, trying to turn the inconvenience of our break-down into a pleasing, social respite.

But the heat bore down like a heavy hand and, within minutes, we were conscious of a thick-tongued thirst. Around us for miles lay nothing but rugged rocks and sun-burned bush. Then Ahmed remembered the car radio and tuned it to a disc jockey show from Radio Tangier. "I will dance for you," he said excitedly. And there, on the remote mountain road, he danced first a mad rock 'n roll, then a kind of samba-rhumba, followed by a variety of other steps, until finally the radio played a waltz. Ahmed, eyes closed in rapture, the perspiration running down to his white collar, did an exaggerated, swooping waltz over the roadbed until all of us, road workers included, were dizzy with laughing and the noise of the men's joyous whoopings echoed out over the valley. Ahmed was hot but beaming; he had pleased us again.

Another late afternoon, as we sat sipping mint tea, Ahmed urged us on to some new activity. However, we were already exhausted from camel riding, sight-seeing and the general ardor of absorbing a strange country. "Please don't be like that," he protested and then, inadvertently but amusingly, reversed an old cliche. "Don't be like that. Some of my best friends are *Christians!*"

Ahmed smoked hashish, though not in chain-pipe fashion; just an occasional pipe when he was relaxing. Frequently, in his need to share, he urged us to have a puff or allow him to load a fresh pipe for us. Consistently, we said, "No, thank you." He seemed distressed that we should miss even *one* of life's pleasures and assured us that he would watch over us like a mother. If the hashish proved too strong, he would take the pipe away immediately. "You will enjoy it," he said warmly and then, obviously trying to think of something that would intrigue an American, "Just three puffs," he said persuasively. "Make you dream *Cadillacs!*"

It was through Ahmed that we went to our first Moroccan wedding. One of his boyhood chums was the groom and, as Ahmed's guests, we were the only females present at the ceremony, held at the bridegroom's home. Just before entering the house, Ahmed warned us, "Don't let anyone know you speak anything but *English!*" (I speak Spanish and our companion spoke excellent French). Through the evening, we were introduced to a series of dignified Arab elders, who bowed, said a few words in Arabic and then left us in friendly silence. For us, our *pose* had an ominous quality, out of keeping with the festive mood of the wedding, but we felt that, for political reasons or something *important,* Ahmed wanted our silence.

Finally, halfway through the evening, I whispered to him, "Why *can't* we talk?"

"Oh, don't talk to them," he urged again. "Then they will try to be polite and make conversation. They will ask you such silly things as how tall are your buildings? How is your president today? Did you know Gary Cooper? Please don't talk! There is nothing more boring to me than a courteous Arab!"

Through that first week of our friendship, Ahmed discussed himself in an urgent, touching fashion. He seemed to want us to know all about his country and customs, to realize that *they* might be different but that *he* was like us. He wanted no mistake made—and certainly his attitude was conditioned by long years of second-class citizenship under French rule. We must realize that he was a good and honest man. And finally he proved it.

On a visit to a mountain village, we saw and wanted to buy a Berber wedding belt, a piece of cloth about eighteen feet long and a yard in width. It was brilliant red wool, fringed and spotted with yellow. Ahmed said he would ask if we might purchase one. After several inquiries, he reported that there were not any for sale. Each new bride wove her own, brought it into town to be dyed and then wore it for the rest of her married life. But finally he arranged for an old village woman to weave one for us. It would take a month or more and cost $18. The time was long and the price high, but we gave Ahmed the money and waited while he darted down a little street. Shortly afterward, we left Morocco and went back to Spain.

For three months, we had no word from our guide. The eighteen dollars and the wedding belt seemed a loss. Then a telegram arrived for us in Spain. Ahmed was arriving by plane on Sunday afternoon. The day was swelteringly hot as he walked up our garden path, perspiring profusely and pale in a heavy Western-type suit. The wedding belt was wrapped in newspaper and string, making a bundle so bulky that he circled it with both arms. Suddenly, Ahmed's gold teeth shone in a smile. He put his package on the ground and mopped his face, breathing deeply, like a man who felt faint.

"Next time you hear 'never trust an Arab,' you tell everybody about Ahmed," he said.

««««««««« »»»»»»»»»

Travel in Morocco is peaceable enough today but tourists are warned (even as in the United States) not to pick up hitchhikers. However, one day, just outside the near-desert town of Taouradant, we were flagged down by a giant Moroccan teen-ager, wearing the uniform of the International Boy Scouts. Again, the skies were scorching and the afternoon too hot to allow anyone to trudge along the road. The young man hopped gratefully into the back seat. He spoke nothing but Arabic, pointing ahead and counting off kilometres on his right hand to indicate his destination.

For several miles he rode in silence and then, in the rear-view mirror, I saw him fumbling excitedly with a long, sheathed knife. A wary tension grew in the front seat. Finally, the young man extracted a bit of paper that had been tucked in the knife-sheath and handed it over to the front seat. He had lost three fingers in an accident, the note said in French, and deserved alms. We delivered him to the spot in the road he indicated and gave him five hundred francs. He thanked us warmly, in true Scout fashion, dusted off the car radiator with his neckerchief and waved good-by.

Even in Morocco, Boy Scouts do their good deed per day.

««««««««« »»»»»»»»»

Juvenile delinquency is something of a problem in this country, but it is a rather special problem. The most common juvenile crime is stealing, and, most frequently, the young thief is poor, unemployed and hungry. Responsible older Arabs are distinctly saddened that conditions sometimes tempt the young to do wrong. In the *souk* section of Casablanca, we were stopped on three separate occasions by dignified Arab men who suggested that we put our wallet in an "inside pocket." (The wallet was, in fact, a leather mapcase which protruded from a jacket pocket.) Each explained similarly, and with apology, that he "regretted this warning was necessary."

At one street corner, a rough-looking teen-aged boy, barefooted and wearing a tattered knit skullcap, stopped us to ask for money, after which he tagged along behind us in a threatening fashion. A stocky, heavily-veiled woman viewed the scene and then stepped forward to give the poor chap a swinging, resounding crack on the ear, followed by a torrent of rapid Arabic. A friend translated: "Let me catch you bothering people again, Ahmed Bouih, and I'll march you home by your ear and tell your *mother!*"

«««««««« »»»»»»»»

Every big Moroccan city has its share of "street boys," teenagers without training or education who make a few francs a day by running errands, peddling peanuts or helping load and unload market stuffs. Some are honestly hard-working; some are just looking for a pleasant way to spend a warm day.

In Tangier, we met one of the latter, a delightfully vague and impractical "guide" who called himself Pinky. This Pinky was small and delicate and, as he sat enshrouded in his *djellaba* on the sidewalk in front of the Hotel Velasquez, he looked more like a heap of clean rags than a human being. But when he saw we had noticed him, he swarmed to his feet, and, with a touchingly loving smile, insisted that he be allowed the honor of showing us his city.

First, he wanted to know if we would like to buy a diamond ring. We told him no. He sighed, then grinned at us. "I could go to the beach and find you one, maybe," he said, this being a slight variation of the oldest and most shopworn selling pitch used by "street boys." Pinky was laughing at himself; laughing at us; laughing at the old, familiar nonsense of humanity. He knew that no one ever found a valuable ring on the beach. Everybody knew this. But tourists could be found who would buy these "diamonds." This was what struck him as funny; the absurdity of the story, and the absurdity of those who bought it.

He turned out to be a charming companion, full of misinformation, garbled facts, preposterous lies. He trotted beside us like a character from the *Arabian Nights,* delightful, incredible, gay. Pinky claimed to be nineteen, but his appearance and imagination were more like those of a boy of ten.

"Bad house there," he said in the casbah, pointing to what was probably the very proper residence of a very proper merchant. "Man kill all his wives. Chop off heads. Bad house." He pointed out donkeys "who come from country," innumerable ragged urchins as "friend from my street." He chattered about trivialities like a third grader, saying everything and anything to hold our attention.

At lunchtime he disappeared, after telling us he "must go home and eat with Mama." We met him hours later, drifting through the streets in a gay fog of hashish. But he remembered us and accompanied us to our hotel, saying happily but vaguely, "Very good day, no?" And then he sank back to his resting place on the sidewalk in front of the hotel. "Be kind to Pinky," he murmured in his last waking moments.

«««««««« »»»»»»»»

Jasmina Naciri was eighteen years old when we met her, but she looked younger, partly because her delicate little face was without make-up and partly because she seemed frightened. Jasmina was desperately eager to talk with American journalists, although she knew her parents would disapprove. We met in the apartment of a friend and in the public park, which gave our talks a secretive quality.

Jasmina is one of the few Moslem girls in Tangier who goes unveiled and wears Western dress. And she is a high-school graduate, having finished four years at one of the big public schools of the city. The strong determination to "go modern and help other Moroccan women" does not show in her gentle, ultra-female face and soft voice.

Jasmina talked in good, schoolgirl English. She also speaks French, Spanish and Arabic. "One day when I was twelve years old, I decided to keep a diary," she told us. "And I have written in it every day since. My first words in that diary were 'Today I am angry. I cannot go out. I want to be free.' "

"I remember that day very clearly. We were living then in the *casbah*. A younger girl friend of mine was having a birthday party in her home and I was invited. And I wanted to go very much. It happened that, although I was twelve years old, my parents had not yet insisted that I wear a veil. They thought I was pretty and just didn't want me to cover my face. Yet my mother herself is always veiled in public. However, I am an only child and they rather spoil me.

"But on the day of that birthday party my mother said to me for the first time, 'Jasmina, you cannot go out today. It is not safe for you nor good for your reputation to be seen on the streets so often. From now on, you must stay home with us. I want people to think of you as a nice girl!'

"I stayed home that day and began my diary. Even though I couldn't go to the birthday party, I knew I still had a better life than some of my friends. . . .

"I had my first wish when my parents did not insist on the veil," explained Jasmina, "But I had to *beg* for my second wish—an education. We are poor people—my father is a taxi driver—and many poor people do not send their children to school at all—especially girls. But I begged my parents to let me go to one of the big public schools in town—the same as your high school, I think. I studied with Arab, French, English and Spanish students."

Jasmina fingered the little string of pearls that trimmed her simple green and brown silk jersey dress. "You will think all Arab girls talk too much," she said with a laugh, before continuing.

"Now I go to a private school in the morning. It is taught by an English woman for students who want to study languages and literature. I pay nine dollars a month to go to this school. Last night, I put something in my diary about my studies. I wrote that I like the plays of Oscar Wilde very much—and I will always judge a writer by his work, not his private life!

"In the afternoon, I have a job as a secretary with the city government of Tangier," she said proudly. "I learned to type in school and I am the only Arab girl employed by the city. My parents were kind about this, too. It's completely against tradition for an Arab girl to work outside the home. I earn about seventy-five dollars a month and give it all to my father. Then he gives me back the money I need for school and clothes. The rest he is saving for his life's dream—to build a little villa of his own in the country before he dies.

"Even though I have freedom to work and study," said Jasmina a little sadly, "I have little freedom in other things. About once a week I go to the library. Other times, I am at home with my parents. But I read and study for nearly three hours at night—so I am busy. I am *learning*—and I have been spared that lifetime prison sentence of the face veil.

"I mean it when I say I want to see the world and know more about other people. I love my country but we must change and we have a lot to learn. I want to write, so other Moroccan women can read and find out how to have a free life. We need a chance—especially the young people. . . ."

All over Morocco, one suspects, there are thousands of teen-aged girls burning with drive and a desire for education and change, other Jasminas still hidden behind thick white walls and thin white veils.

«««««««« »»»»»»»»

One afternoon, in the market of Casablanca, we talked with a young and pleasant Arab about Allah. He was pleased to discuss this; he seemed delighted that we had brought up the subject. His dark eyes became excited, and a fond smile touched his lips, as if we had asked him about a particularly dear friend. We had queried him simply about why his conversation was so thickly sprinkled with references to "God"—"in the name of Allah," "go with Allah," "if Allah wills it," etc.

"Why do we say 'Allah' so much of the time during the day? It is not exactly like a prayer," he explained. "It is freer than that. If something funny happens, we mention it to Allah so he can share the joke. We talk over our problems with him, not always as our God, but as a dear friend and companion who is walking beside us in our journey through life. He is always nearby. . . ."

««««««««« »»»»»»»»»

Chauen is a rugged, remote mountain town which, till about thirty-five years ago, had not known the tread of a Christian foot. It is isolated in time and space, almost without contact with the twentieth century. Roads leading to it are rough and rocky; the surrounding countryside is a masterpiece of isolated peaks and remote valleys. The little streets of Chauen twist and dip, often slippery with human offal. The houses are whitewashed or painted a whimsical springtime blue. Berber farmers from the hillsides fill the town, jogging in on little donkeys or covering the mountain miles on leather-soled feet.

It was here I met my favorite female "Berber friend." At high noon, the dark little cupboardlike shops of the *souk* were closed for lunch or siesta. In the interior darkness, one could see the shopkeepers napping under their *burnooses,* or taking time out for a noontime glass of tea, kettles simmering on tiny braziers. Outside one booth in which the proprietor dozed, hung a bunch of gay red wool cords, tied together in threes in an intricate system of colored knots.

I was by myself, sight-seeing languidly, more interested in looking than buying. Curious, I took one of the wool "harnesses" from its hook and tied it around my waist as a belt. Obviously, it was meant for something else. At that moment, I must have looked puzzled.

A young Berber tribeswoman, a traveler in from the mountains, stepped over to my side. With a smile, she took the cords from my hand. She was young, I know, in spite of her harshly weathered skin. Her cheekbones and nose were as distinctive as an American Indian's. The woman's body was swathed in the hand-woven red and white striping of the mountain people, her ankles cased in leather sheathing and her heavy, work-broadened wrists ringed in coarse silver. Three blue dots were tattoed down her forehead and three more from the lower lip down the chin. Against the sun, she wore a cartwheel straw hat, its crown decorated with colored wool bobbles and glinting bits of mirror. Animated and decorated as she was, one might guess she easily rated as a belle of her tribe.

Pantomiming as cleverly and adroitly as Red Skelton, this Berber showed me how the *harness* should be worn. In her play-acting, she was first a gay young female, using the red cords to carry burdens on her back. Next this gay young thing became heavy with child, the burdens still on her back, when the child was born. It joined the burdens which a woman must always carry on her shoulders, child *and* bundles, held in place by the colored cording.

It was a charmingly intimate and unself-conscious performance. The young Berber's face was full of friendliness and an explosive good-humor. Her white teeth, rugged as those of a healthy horse, flashed in smiles. We were from different worlds but she knew that, as a woman, I would understand: *women, babies, burdens—always.*

«««««««« »»»»»»»»

In Marrakesh we arranged for a guided tour of the historic sites. Promptly at nine the following morning, our guide arrived, a tall and handsome Arab in his forties, impeccably turned out in a red *fez* and light blue *djellaba,* worn over a gray business suit. His manner was cold, stern, aloof. We drove to the old palace in silence. Once or twice, in answer to a direct question, he would provide information about our route: "That is the Administration Building" or "There is the route to the Atlas Mountains." He delivered these lines in a stiff, disinterested voice. At the palace and later at the casbah, he was no better. Finally, we said, in effect, "What's the matter? Have you seen this so often that it no longer interests you?"

It triggered an outburst. "*Interests me?* It is my *life!* It is my country, a free country, but we are still too much ruled by the French. For years we are nothing to them but Arab, dirty Arab! Now they have broken promises about money, about help. Each year our anger, our frustration grows." Now he seemed more relaxed. He smiled tentatively at us. "We take out our bad feelings on all foreigners. You must forgive me."

The rest of the day was spent in a routinely good-natured manner but one of the guide's comments is worth underscoring and remembering. "France is for Frenchmen, England is for the English," he said. "Spain is for the Spaniards. It's Allah's way. And thus Algeria must be for Arabs, Morocco must be for Arabs, Tunisia, Egypt—*all of it*—must be for Arabs!"

Here was a man who had recently seen his own country's freedom emerge in triumph, ruthlessly stepping over the borders of other independent lands.

«««««««« »»»»»»»»

Princess Aisha, the eldest daughter of the Moroccan royal family, is a beautiful young woman, dark-eyed, intense and graceful. Her skin is fair, tanned lightly by the sun, her warm, full mouth is often touched by a shy smile. Her face, elegant but compassionate, is known throughout Morocco—not only for its celebrity value and beauty but because it has been *photographed and seen.*

This diminutive princess has chosen to break a 1300-year old tradition among Moroccan women by publically and permanently discarding her face veil.

To some conservative Moroccans, Lalla Aisha (Lalla means Princess) is an insult to the Prophet. To others, she is simply "the Princess—who can do whatever she likes." But to increasing thousands of young girls and to freedom-stirred women, this princess is a victory figure, a champion of change, the woman who may lead all Moroccan women into a more modern way of life. Many teen-aged girl students, unveiled and free to go to school for the first time, carry a small photograph of Aisha in their school-uniform pockets, over the heart, as daily inspiration.

Earliest pictures of Lalla Aisha show her as a merry-faced, chubby child, her short, dark hair bound up with silver filigree, her tiny body swathed in long silken and embroidered gowns, girded and jangling with the jewels and trappings of princesshood. On state occasions, in her pre-teen years, she was a solemn little figure. In her pictures, she is always grave, poised and attentive, her sensitive face seemingly reflecting the serious responsibilities of being a princess.

As the first daughter, she was long her father's favorite companion. The tile-floored halls of the Rabat palace screeched with the wheels of her tiny tricycle; shiploads of toys were brought in from Paris for her nursery. It was for her that the former King Mohammed built tennis courts and a private swimming pool, and for her that French governesses were allowed to live within the palace walls. And it was at his thoughtful and solemn urging that she decided to abandon the veil, make public speeches and preside at the openings of orphanages, bazaars and fund drives, like a western-world princess. Several years ago, Lalla Aisha came to the United States as her father's emissary, appearing at state dinners and Washington parties in chic Paris gowns. Once she withdrew from the royal party, though carefully chaperoned, to have dinner with an ex-Moroccan, now a cab driver in Brooklyn.

On the whole, hers has been a modified leadership, a female emergence that was dignified and nonmilitant and hence could give courage to Moroccan females with a minimum of offense to tradition.

But the confines of custom have not yet released Lalla Aisha completely. At thirty, she still lives in the family palace and is still unmarried. Why? Because, say her friends, it is not possible for her to meet and get to know eligible men who would propose marriage to a "free princess." Never is she allowed in the company of males without one of her brothers or several female companions present. And never is she allowed to dine, even at the palace of a brother, when unmarried men are present.

"She must wait, like most of us," explained a young Moroccan woman, "until some man asks her brother, the King, for her hand. And who would dare to ask for the hand of the Princess?" So far—no one.

And so the lights in Princess Aisha's palace apartment burn long into the night, as she whiles away the late evenings alone, reading voraciously or listening to music. Lalla Aisha has gained many freedoms for other Moroccan women but for herself she has not yet gained the freedom to become a full and beloved woman.

«««««««« »»»»»»»»

On February 26, 1961, a warm and peaceful day in Morocco, the news of a stunning tragedy sped through the country. King Mohammed V was dead. A minor nasal operation, with complications, took the life of the fifty-two-year-old leader who had guided his country from French domination into full and promising freedom.

Immediately after the death announcement, the King's eldest son, Moulay Hassan, was proclaimed King Hassan II. But there was little joy. The country was plunged into seven days of genuine, heartfelt mourning. Thousands jammed highways and country roads to reach Rabat in time to file past the bier of their dead king. All cafes, cinemas and other places of entertainment were closed; the red and green national flag flew at half mast. Around the palace walls, crowds pressed close, moaning and crying. Mosques everywhere were filled and, in towns and villages, hundreds marched through the streets, reciting en masse prayers for the dead from the Koran. Veiled women scratched at their cheeks and foreheads until the blood ran, an ages-old Moroccan custom of mourning.

Who was this man who could send ten million people into such a frenzy of sadness? King Mohammed V, known as Ben Youssef in his earlier years, had been appointed as puppet sultan by the French in 1927, when he was only seventeen. At the death of his father, the then reigning sultan, he was selected over his older brother because the French believed Ben Youssef to be an easy-to-handle lightweight. He was known as a fair tennis player, a skillful horseman and lover of fast cars. In short, thought the French, he was a harmless playboy.

But maturity brought a seriousness of purpose and personal strength to Ben Youssef. His ancestry traced back to Ali, son-in-law of the founder of Islam, the Prophet Mohammed, and he was considered the spiritual as well as the political leader of Morocco. A devout Moslem, he abstained from all alcohol, observed religious customs faithfully and spent at least an hour a day reading the Koran. Also, he was a loving and responsible family man, with two wives and two sons and four daughters, all six children by the first wife.

Many observers believe that the Sultan's first strong determination to win independence for his country stemmed from a meeting with United States President, Franklin D. Roosevelt, at a World War II conference in Casablanca. The two met privately, without French officials present, and Ben Youssef experienced for the first time the dignity of being treated as a true head of state. In 1945, he initially alarmed the French and alerted them to his intentions by proclaiming in a public speech, "The protectorate regime is a suit tailored for Morocco in 1912. In 1945, it barely reaches to the knees."

Local uprisings and agitations became so frequent and troublesome to the French regime that, in 1953, it was decided Sultan Ben Youssef had to go. He was roused from a summer-day siesta by French officials and marched to an airplane while still in his pajamas. For two years, he was held in exile on the island of Madagascar. At that time his most powerful weapon, it is said, was the constant refusal to use his influence to quell the bloody riots now gravely troubling French control in Morocco. Ben Youssef's ideas and strength of leadership filtered down to his people.

In 1955, he was returned from exile and remounted on the throne; in 1956, Morocco was declared independent. The same people of Morocco who had cheered the proclamation that Ben Youssef was now King Mohammed V had good reason to bewail his death. They had lost both a leader and a loved father-image; their tears and prayers were genuine.

«««««««« »»»»»»»»

King Moulay Hassan II was thirty-one years old when he became political and spiritual leader of all Morocco. He is a short, dark-haired young man who is as handsome as a movie star. Closely associated with his father in government for years, he was acting Premier as well as Crown Prince at the time of Mohammed V's death. Non-Moroccan publications have long associated him with beach parties, sports cars, French movie starlets and the high and easy life. (Moulay Hassan, then Crown Prince, was once pointed out to me at a Casablanca cocktail party given by a French sugar merchant. He was indeed handsome, dressed in a navy blue pin-striped suit, chatting in French and sipping a soft drink.) Insiders say he is a determined young man, educated as a lawyer, and fully cognizant of the responsibilities that lie on his young shoulders. Hassen has not yet married but is expected to pick a bride soon, since bachelorhood is not considered seemly for the spiritual leader of the kingdom. For a number of years he has maintained a lush private villa outside the palace walls, commuting to his offices each day like a working politician.

He believes in a strong monarchy, with "a team of responsible men grouped around a chief, capable of giving the powerful impetus necessary to lead the people in their fight for progress and against poverty."

His father died on a Sunday and on Monday King Hassan followed the funeral procession through the Rabat streets on foot, chanting the traditional prayers. Two days later, he granted an interview to the local press in which he said, "In this period of uncertainty, of struggle against underdevelopment, of lack of trained cadres, the people need a man in whom they have confidence."

Next day, he held meetings with political leaders from nearby Algeria and Tunisia.

On Friday, the Holy Day, wearing voluminous robes and

imitating, said the newspapers, his father's serene gestures, he rode to a mosque to lead the faithful in sabbath prayers.

In five days, this young man had taken over his roles as both political and spiritual leader. Morocco will long remember King Mohammed V but—the old King is dead, long live King Hassan II!

Chapter III

MUTTON, MELONS AND HOT MINT TEA

THE WORD "food" conjures up a different picture for every country in the world. When food is plentiful, it is a vital picture, with varied colors, textures and distinctive smells. And in that picture we see not only food but bits of information about the people who eat it—their work and income and their way of life, the climate and condition of the land.

In the United States, we can think of food nationally—thick steaks with French fries, hot dogs and mustard at the ball park, backyard barbecues and strawberry shortcake in the springtime. There are regional favorites, of course, such as baked beans around Boston, hot tamales in Texas, southern fried chicken in Alabama or cold, cracked crab served near the docks in San Francisco.

But, in general, most of us throughout the entire country would probably pick the *same* foods and the *same* brand-names as sounding—and tasting—typically "American." We could conjure up identical pictures of bottled soft drinks, sugar-crisped cereals, pasteurized milk delivered to the door or fresh-frozen vegetables in uniform-sized packages. A big supermarket with its wire shopping carts, well-stocked, self-service shelves and soft, piped-in music is essentially the same in Louisville, Kentucky and in Cheyenne, Wyoming. Our prosperity and our tastes—and much about Americans as people—show through our eating and shopping habits.

How would the "food picture" look in Morocco? If it were a still life, that picture would have to have a freshly-killed chicken, waiting to be plucked, a few paper twists of spices, a melon cooling under damp straw and a bunch of green mint, as fresh as mountain dew. And if the picture is to be a more active, populated canvas, we must start with a market place, exactly the sort of place where so many Moroccans start their day.

About eighty-five per cent of the people of this country make their livelihood from agriculture, producing such crops as cereals, citrus and other fruits, green vegetables, olives, almonds and some livestock. In getting the whole picture of the food habits of the country, it is important to remember that, outside of hotels and French or exceedingly prosperous Arab homes, there is little refrigeration. Hence there is a constant flow of traffic in the supply and demand for food. During most of the daylight hours, the immediate roads outside towns and villages look like endless circus parades, with donkeys and camels trekking to or from market, with panniers of supplies, charcoal for cooking, hay for other animals—and human cargo, too, hitching a ride. And since most markets are held outdoors, food and the work connected with it seem to be constantly in evidence in Morocco.

«««««««« »»»»»»»»

In the more sparsely populated countryside, market day falls once a week, when the local farmers bring their produce to a trading spot, housed for that day under sagging, striped tents. In the big cities, every day is market day, except Friday (the Moslem Holy Day) when stalls are shut tight and the cobblestoned streets are quiet. Markets come awake at dawn, when the merchants begin to arrange their wares and the first donkeys appear, ticktacking in from the hills. Closing hours arrive with dusk and the last housewife's tucking a bit of stew meat in her shopping basket.

The mood of the market is social; for a people who rarely read a newspaper, it is a time to exchange national and local gossip. The Berber women, always unveiled and with faces wrinkled by smiles and rough mountain weather, are loud, good-natured talkers, and even the veiled Arab women like to pause a moment to whisper about neighborhood news. Coming from country-far distances, many Berber women bring their infants, slung to the back in a snood of red and white cloth. The companionship and the confusion of the market place, or *souk,* keep the little ones happy all day. Many children nap on straw matting under the make-shift counters while their mothers hawk vegetables or melons. A sweet date or soft peach, slipped under the counter, can still any restless cry. At night, the small children sleep soundly on the long walk home, lulled by the rhythms of mothers' bodies as they trudge up hills and along winding roads.

In the very early hours, the market is just a gray, ramshackle collection of warped wooden booths and sheet-iron counters, open to the street and covering blocks and blocks in the heart of the city. Some booths have padlocked doors so goods may be stored safely inside, but most food supplies are delivered fresh and the counters are restocked each day. By noontime, the market is a bedlam of commerce, pungent with fruity and spicey smells and brilliant with color.

A representative example of a big-city market is the *socco* of Tangier, located in the heart of the city, edged on one side by the cosmopolitan section of town and merging on the other three into the casbah. The city's leading synagogue is here, as are two Catholic churches and several smaller mosques.

«««««««« »»»»»»»»

In the *souks,* most foodstuffs are divided into areas, so that butchers occupy one street, fruitiers another, vegetable vendors another, while the flower sellers make a bouquet of booths all by themselves. The fish market is always easy to find, not only by the distinctive odor of fish-heads and scales drying on the pavement, but by the dozens of huge cats perched on the roofs of the booths, tails flexing patiently in the sun, waiting for the day-end feast of scraps. So much of Morocco is bordered by seacoast that the fish supply is plentiful and good—and cheaper than most meats. The selections from the deep run from the pinkish, babies'-fingers tangle of young squid to great slabs of Atlantic tuna, looking as stalwart and protein-packed as sides of young beef.

Vegetables are plentiful year-round and the most common are onions, peppers, tomatoes, garlic buds, squashes, potatoes and leafy greens. Very little corn was grown in Morocco until recently, when an American woman, married to a Spaniard, began experimenting with it on the northern plains. With vegetables, as with most other foodstuffs, the housewife shops by the day, taking two green peppers now, half a dozen potatoes, an onion or two—all weighed carefully on a rusty scale-and-balance, right before her watchful eyes. Moroccans are canny budgeters and bargainers and it is common for a woman to bargain for six tomatoes at this booth, then try her luck at the next and the next, returning at last to the merchant who has given her the best price. This bargaining, too, is "social," a pastime enjoyed by both buyer and seller.

Fruits run the whole warm-country gamut, with the exception of bananas and pineapples, which are luxuries. But booths and vendors' baskets are piled high with apples, peaches, grapes, pears, melons and citrus fruits. The Moroccan cantaloupes are about as big as an indoor baseball and sweetly succulent. A Moroccan special in the fruit market is the pinkish-green cactus pear, cut from the paddle cactus. This is thorny-skinned and must be peeled to get at the stringy, ultrasweet flesh. It is inexpensive, often gathered wild from cacti growing along the roadside and carted to market by ragged Berber children who peddle one fruit, plus a drink of water, for about a penny. Dates are trucked or camel-packed in from southern Morocco and are sold soft and sticky-fresh or dried into blocks so hard that they must be hacked off with a sharp knife. Dried dates, incidentally, are often carried by shepherds or country-travelers, just as the American Indians once packed *pemmican* or soldiers hardtack, to be gnawed at whenever hunger pangs strike.

Since many of the merchants are small-timers or farmers' wives in town with a single basket of produce to sell, competition is high and all wares are displayed as appealingly as possible. In the leisurely early hours, merchants busy themselves arranging the fruits and vegetables in attractive rows or pyramids, dusting an apple here and snipping off bruised grapes there. Seated on the sidewalk, her simple wares arranged on a straw mat, a woman may shift, judge and rearrange her food display as critically as a Fifth Avenue window dresser. In the heat of the day, the produce gets frequent sprinklings of water, sloshed by hand from a bucket, to give it the freshness of garden dew. But no amount of sprinkling or fanning can keep away the tiny bees that swarm over every bit of bruised fruit and make a constant buzzing haze over the mounds of dates, fresh or dried.

Moroccans love flowers and the flower stalls do a brisk business, even if a day's purchase is only three phlox and two roses. In the early springtime, almost every country field is colored with daisies and red poppies but the market flowers are raised by local farmers, with as much care as they employ in tending their grapes and peaches. Certain species of roses, jasmine and geranium are highly scented and the Moroccan housewife may crush a flower along a bedroom doorsill, on a pillow or around a dinner tray for its special fragrance.

«««««««« »»»»»»»»

Chicken and sheep (lamb or mutton) are the favorite meats in this country and again, without refrigeration, these are usually bought in small quantity and just for the day. Most chickens, in fact, make that trek from the market to the kitchen guillotine, still alive, feet tied together and beady eyes peeking out of straw shopping baskets. Frequently, the roosters and older birds are tethered along the sidewalk by one leg, squawking and fighting away their last hours in indignation and rancor. Many a "merchant" in the poultry section is an ancient farmer who has shuffled into town with three or four birds. He seats himself against a sunny wall, arranges his hobbled fowl on the usual straw mats—and waits. If the day is hot and customers few, both merchant and fowl nap together, birds with heads tucked under a wing, old man hooded discreetly under a fold of his *djellaba.*

Butchers' stands are usually unscreened and open to the street, with sides of meat and smaller pieces of flesh hanging on hooks, waiting to be sectioned on order. Often it is a close race between the flies and the housewives to get a choice piece.

Beggars frequently make the rounds of the market, stopping at each butcher's stall to make a plea in the name of Allah. Naturally, each prayer is answered, usually with a thin sliver of meat, which the mendicant adds to his begging dish, collecting enough bits of lamb, liver, oxtail and beef scraps through the day to simmer up a tasty stew.

A certain meat market scene has stuck in my mind for years, and *not* because it was unpleasant: in the *souk* of Marrakesh, one noontime, we spotted three ragged beggars huddled cross-legged under a butcher's counter. The butcher had dropped them some tiny bits of meat and the old fellows were curled up cross-legged, chatting and "roasting" the fleshy fragments over the low glow of their hashish pipes, turning and roasting the bits like fastidious chefs and thoroughly relishing the scanty meal. A very odd background, a very odd menu—but those beggars were savoring the best part of any meal: good talk and companionship.

«««««««« »»»»»»»»

Somewhere between the fruit and the flowers, one finds the stalls which sell the magnificent Moroccan mint, the basis of the country's national drink, mint tea. This mint is long-stemmed, heavily foliaged, bright green and highly flavored and scented; in short, it is probably the *mintiest* mint in the world. I asked a Moroccan farmer one day what special type of cultivation made his mint so good and he answered that the mint "is surely a gift from Allah." Where else on earth could mint grow in the blazing sun by day and be refurbished and flavored by the cool, irrigating dews of the night?

Moroccans love mint tea because of its fresh taste and the

energy derived from the sugar and because, served hot, it is cooling, even on a broiling day. It is also the nation's hospitality symbol and is drunk almost anywhere, at any hour, where friend meets friend.

There are as many theories about how to make a good glass of mint tea as there are cooks' speculations about a perfect piecrust. And the results vary. At a roadside stand, where the charcoal brazier is burning low, one may be served a tepid, sea-green glassful, almost like sweetened water; again, a wealthy and meticulous host will make the tea for guests himself, giving it the care of a connoisseur. I watched our host make tea at his home one evening in Rabat and put down *his* method as the best:

A medium-sized brass pot (to serve six) is stuffed with a few sprigs of fresh mint, then filled with boiling water and left to stand. In three or four minutes, the contents of the pot is removed, leaving the metal heated by the water and cleansed of any "taste" by the mint. Now a generous handful of fresh mint is stuffed into the pot and pressed down, to break a few leaves; next the tea is spooned in. Now add about six lumps of fine sugar and another arrangement of mint leaves. *Now* fill to the top with fresh boiling water and let stand five minutes. Our host sampled the tea first himself, pouring a little into a glass and taking a sip. It took three such samplings before he felt the beverage was perfect for us. It was: steaming hot, thickly sugared and heavily flavored with mint.

This tea, incidentally, is always served in a glass and, since it is usually so hot, must be held by the rim and bottom of the glass, thumb at the bottom, middle finger on the rim. Some cafes add a decorative sprig of fresh mint to each glass but the purists feel that, once the tea is poured from the pot, it is "in the hands of Allah" and ready to drink.

I was amused to see that Moroccan workers enjoy a "mint tea break," just as we like a "coffee break" in the United States. When it is not convenient to go to a café, peddlers may stop their donkeys or mechanics will roll out from under cars to buy a glass of tea from a little boy, radiating out from a local café with his wares, carrying the glasses of hot tea in a wire frame like a multiple-eggholder.

Incidentally, every market place is ringed with small cafes selling mint tea and soft drinks, and male merchants and shoppers often lounge over a soothing glass, talking and listening to the inevitable radio blaring in the background—but Moslem *women,* never. A woman shopper must bear the burdens of heavy baskets, a baby and perhaps a live chicken and a load of kindling without any pause for refreshment. It would just not be proper.

«««««««« »»»»»»»»

Here are three typically Moroccan "sights of the souk" that deserve special note. Fresh goat's milk is always available. Why? Because a shepherd simply leads his goat to market, finds a shady corner and sets up business, milking the goat on the spot for each customer. Many of these goats are brown and white, marked curiously so that the color line runs around the breadth of the body, dividing the animal almost exactly into two colors. But all the milk comes out in the natural thick, creamy beige of regular goats' milk.

The market place is also the gathering spot for the public letter writers, who cluster close to the gates or bus stops, eager to read or write letters for a fee. Their props of pen, inkpot and paper are ranged before them on a straw mat and, whether or not they are truly deep thinkers, these men usually have a detached, preoccupied air. For a fee, they will also read the daily paper to a group.

In the larger cities, with improved water systems, water-vendors are becoming scarce but they still roam the smaller markets, usually ragged chaps wearing huge straw hats hung with bobbles and carting goatskin water bags across their shoulders. A brace of tin cups hangs from one wrist and the shoulder harness is strung with little bells, both for advertising and to scare off any evil spirit which might contaminate the water.

«««««««« »»»»»»»»

Moroccans enjoy well-seasoned food, so the spice merchants form a special part of any market, their displays as colorful and dustily fragrant as powdered flowers. The spices are arranged in bulky heaps and include yellow saffron, black pepper, brown cinnamon, red papkrika and dozens of others. In Tangier, one section of the spice market is laid out along a broad flight of public steps, one merchant to each step with his displays circled around him, so that the stairs seem to be carpeted in exotic piles and colors. Wrapping paper is scarce and expensive here, so most spices are sold by the spoonful, then wrapped in squares of newspaper or pages from old magazines or school copybooks. I bought a potpourri of spices, the special combination necessary for *herrira* soup, and the merchant twisted it in tablet paper on which some student had once written a school assignment—the story of Goldilocks and the three bears in careful French!

«««««««« »»»»»»»»

Perhaps *hashish* does not fit into the Moroccan shopping basket every day but it *is* sold in the open market and it is used frequently by men all over Morocco. *Hashish,* made from the top leaves and tender parts of Indian hemp, is dried for both smoking and chewing. In this form, it has "intoxicating qualities"; in short, *hashish* is mild dope. In the *souk,* it can be bought economically in the uncrushed, dried flower stage. It is more expensive when prepared and powdered down. My interest and curiosity was aroused by a popular sweetmeat called "hashish fudge." A Moroccan friend once gave me a small gift box of this fudge which I carried unsampled in a suitcase pocket till it finally merged with the colognes, travel booklets and pop-it pearls. But it looked and smelled like dried, pressed raisins and is made this way:

"Take one teaspoon of black peppercorns, one whole nutmeg, four average sticks of cinnamon and one teaspoon of coriander and pulverize them in a mortar. Then take about one handful each of stoned dates, dried figs, shelled almonds and peanuts and chop them up and mix them together. Then take two ounces or so of pulverized Cannibas Sativa (hashish) and the spices and knead them together with the mixed fruits and nuts and with about a cup of sugar dissolved in a big pat of butter. The whole is then rolled into a cake and cut into pieces or made into balls about the size of a walnut."

To this I would add, "eat fresh—if you eat at all!" Regardless of its interesting properties as a stimulant, my preserved fudge would have been a tooth-cracker.

«««««««« »»»»»»»»

Crowded between booths here and there in every busy *souk* is the Moroccan version of the snack bar, usually just a hole-in-the wall with a doorway open to the street. Here whole unseeded green peppers, meat balls or tiny lamb chunks (*shishkabob*) are strung on a wire and heated and toasted over a low charcoal fire. I was told that roasted locusts were once popular but I either missed the right season or the taste has faded. Diners stand crowded in the narrow streets, hands carefully cupped to keep the dripping tidbits off the djellabas, while donkeys and basket-laden shoppers jostle from behind. As a refreshing finish, a half-melon from which the proprietor solicitously whisks the bees is always good.

In a sunny, foot-traveling country like Morocco, thirst can often be a major problem and the in-town snack bars diminish in menu and size as the customers filter thinner and thinner into the wastes of the countryside. At great intervals outside the towns one can find ramshackle stands selling water and chilled soft drinks. Farther on, a tiny tent may shelter unchilled bottled drinks—and way out in the remote nowhere, one can see the last of the "thirst merchants," usually an Arab boy dozing in the shade of an isolated tree with a little heap of melons beside him. On a hot day, far from comforts, a melon can be as refreshing as an iced coke.

«««««««« »»»»»»»»

Moroccan restaurants range from the economical to the lavish, though the latter are usually patronized by non-Moroccan businessmen or tourists. Since most Moroccans are genuinely hospitable, it is somewhat rare to find a Moroccan traveler within his own country entertained outside a private home. But there are some good nontourist eating places and we *did* find a modest, back-street restaurant in a casbah one day that provided not only delicious food but two of the most memorable family scenes I remember in all Morocco.

This restaurant was entered through an intricately iron-bound door, the only opening in a high wall facing the street. Inside, the center room was two stories high and sky-lighted, a rendezvous spot for men wanting only mint tea and a quiet hashish pipe. Over the large refrigerator hung a colored oil portrait of King Mohammed the Fifth, head haloed saint-fashion and hands lifted dramatically toward some very yellow, very pointed stars. A radio blared forth loud Arab music, barely drowning out the asthmatic groans of the ancient refrigerator motor.

To one side was a small dining room, decorated shoulder-high with ornate tiles and furnished with low tables, wall couches and bolsters and a few folding chairs. Dim light glimmered down from ceiling lanterns of heavy, cut iron. We were the only foreign customers that day.

Opposite us, against the tiled wall, sat a very young married couple, eating nothing, saying nothing—just sitting together. The boy looked no more than seventeen, simply dressed in coarse brown *djellaba* and colorful knit skullcap. The girl was tiny, wrapped in a dull blue gown and hood, with a white face veil, no features showing but shy, expressive eyes. During our entire lunchtime, they never moved, never even whispered but, beneath the table, one could see their bare ankles just touching, his rough and brown in heelless yellow slippers, hers pale and thin in sandals. And their eyes were cast down to look at their right hands, linked together lightly but so importantly by the little fingers. In the dimness of the restaurant, they were almost like shadows on the wall. What was their story? Did they live in a house so crowded with family and relatives that there was no privacy for young love? Was she the victim of a dominating, stultifying mother-in-law? Or was the marriage still so new, so vital that for these few moments at lunchtime she stole away just to touch his hand? Whatever the story, their quiet happiness touched the whole room.

At the far end of the dining chamber stood a longer table and to this was ushered a trim Moroccan businessman in western dress, several young children and three women, two of the latter stout and one elegantly slim, obviously his three wives. All the women were heavily bundled and veiled. The father picked the head of the table and the women ranged themselves along a wall, after each had settled a child on a straight chair, fussing with pillows and napkin-bibs. The youngest woman, the slim one, then unslung an infant from the coverings on her back and cradled it affectionately on her knees. How would they eat, we wondered, these Moslem women who never—it is said—unveiled their faces in public?

The head of the house ordered for the group: roast lamb with vegetables, some cous-cous—and salad with bread and fruit for the children. The chatter at the table was low and good-natured, the children's behavior impeccable. The infant was discreetly placed under its mother's robes and given a natural lunch. Finally, the food arrived, steaming and succulent, and was served with a clang of brass trays and heavy silverware. And what did the women do? Simply slipped down their veils till they hung under their chins like cowboys' handkerchiefs, exposing their faces completely.

This was the only time, incidentally, that I ever saw three wives of the same husband in Morocco. I was curious as to whether or not their behavior would show jealousy, domination, coquetry or discontent. This trio simply chatted away like warmhearted, good friends, though they were markedly different in age and beauty, marching up the ladder of time in about five-year intervals. The youngest, and probably latest wife, was the slim, nursing mother, an elegantly lovely, simple-faced creature who unveiled the brown, smooth skin of a Negro. And because of the centuries of mixing of blood lines in Morocco, her infant was the same light cream-color as its half-brothers and sister, so calmly using bread crusts to mop up the last of their salads.

«««««««« »»»»»»»»

More elaborate Moroccan restaurants are often located in old, in-town palaces which are excellent examples of Moroccan architecture and furnishings, with arched doorways, carved pillars, intricately tiled floors and walls and great hanging lanterns that cast seductive, fretwork shadows. Wall divans are arranged with soft bolsters for lounging while eating. Tables are always low and illuminated with candles in heavy brass stands. The atmosphere is sultry and relaxed, scented with incense and sandalwood. The dimness of the lights, the obsequious *slip-slip* of the waiters' slippers and the slowness of the service give a calming feeling of dining in a room alone. Certainly the *pashas* who once owned these palaces must have enjoyed their mode of living.

Most restaurants (again emulating a luxurious private home) provide music, usually a four-man orchestra, seated cross-legged on straw matting with such instruments as tambourines, flute-like pipes and finger-drums. The music has a high, skirling quality and the players pause frequently to sip their mint tea or puff the hashish pipes constantly at their knees. Dining hours are late and leisurely in Morocco and the atmosphere at midnight is the same as at eight o'clock.

As part of the "*pasha* mood," dancers present periodic entertainment. These are always boys in their early teens, with bodies as slim and supple as those of graceful girls. Since women are traditionally secluded, boys play the part of female dancers, much as boys played female roles in the days of the Shakespearean theater in England.

The dancers wear tightly-bound, colorful turbans and harem-type pants covered by a full redingote dress that opens and swirls about them with each movement. Feet are bare and the rhythmic *slap-slap* of the soles is an important part of the dancing skill. These dancers usually appear singly or in pairs and the performance consists of sinuous gyrations of the upper and then the lower half of the body, alternately, and slow, graceful movements of the arms and hands. Characteristically, the face stays expressionless, eyes downcast, in imitation of a shy girl. Occasionally, the movements are interspersed with twisting, bending acrobatics, for which the body must be as supple as a snake's. The whole display courses toward a *finale,* with a wild increase in the beat of the music, the movements of the body and the noise of bare feet, until the climax is like watching a human whirlwind.

A specialty of grace and balance is the "tray dance," in which a dancer goes through the rhythms and gyrations of his dance while balancing a huge brass tray on his head. The tray is set with glasses of mint tea and flaming candles and the dance ends with the performer supine on the floor, the tray still in perfect balance.

At village feasts, men and women may take part in the group dances together, and at a pasha's private *diffa* (or feast) the dancers can number into the dozens—but the basic steps and rhythms are always the same, with the accent on suppleness, grace and sensual qualities rather than on formalized steps or joyous patterns.

«««««««« »»»»»»»»

Moroccan food often combines the stimulating qualities of "hot" and "cool" tastes and, without going into the intricacies of actual recipes, here are some of the more delicious Moroccan dishes.

Herrira or Ramadan soup is served most days during the holy month of Ramada, when all good Moslems fast from 4 a.m. to 7 p.m. It is a rich and nourishing soup which can restore both vitality and good tempers very quickly.

The basis is mutton or other stew meat, cut up very small, browned and then cooked with parsley, celery, onions, garlic, tomatoes, flour, beaten eggs and *'smen* (see later) and seasoned with *lekama. Lekama* is spices, bought pre-mixed in the *souk.* Merchants can assemble just the right mixture freehand from long years of experience. It is a combination of black pepper, cloves, saffron, nutmeg, ginger and cinnamon. Each steaming bowl of soup is topped with thin slices of lemon just before serving, to help cool the tongue!

Fish or eggs in hot sauce is a dish common in the south of Spain, as well as in Morocco, and hence it is probably centuries old. And who knows which housewife exchanged the first recipe, Spanish or Berber? The sauce is simply a puree of hot oil, garlic, tomatoes and parsley, well blended. Bits of fish are pre-boiled before adding and eggs are broken into the boiling sauce and served whole.

Pigeon pie is a delicacy so special and so difficult to make that it takes (I've heard) a good Moroccan cook as long as eight hours to make the forty-odd paper-thin layers of pastry to hold the minced pigeon filling. The pigeon is spiced and sometimes mixed with pine nuts or sliced olives and the whole concoction, crust and all, is about an inch high. Served very hot, the pie is sprinkled incongruously—and deliciously—with fine powdered sugar. So succulent is this dish that it seems not to be "eaten" at all; rather it melts in the mouth.

Cous-Cous is indeed the Moroccan national dish, used at every *diffa* and also as the basis of the most simple diets. It can be dressed up or down, depending on the budget and occasion. Cous-cous itself is a seminola made of wheat and it has a rich, cereal taste. Eaten plain, it is heavy and filling; at *diffas,* when it is served with steamed chicken, carrots, onions, raisins and a hot sauce, it becomes almost a gastronomical burden.

The cous-cous is served in a peaked mound, with the additions laid around it or pressed into the soft meal, and kept hot with a pointed hood-covering, either of decorated brass or woven straw.

Lamb can come to the table in many forms. It may be the whole animal, roasted and sprinkled with "kummin" (which, to my surprise, I found in our local supermarket, right next to the garlic salt) or in *shishkabob* form. Whole or half lambs are usually roasted slowly in outdoor ovens made of baked clay until they are tender enough to be pulled apart with the fingers.

Unlike our popular backyard-barbecue *shishkabobs,* which we augment with mushrooms, tomatoes, onions, etc., Moroccan cooks prefer the plain meat, cut into very small squares and strung on iron skewers almost as thin as wire. The lamb is rubbed with a mixture of ground parsley, *kummin* and *lekama* and left to stand for an hour, then roasted quickly over low coals. It is served, still rare inside, with a half lemon for squeezing and a bit of bread for pushing the meat off the skewer and onto the plate.

Chicken, because it can be kept alive and fresh until the last moment, is used frequently and the most unusual chicken dish we sampled was tiny young chickens, roasted whole, and served in a smothering of rich, hot cream to which little stewed peaches had been added. Also delicious is a chicken stew made with olives and lemons.

Desserts are usually simple and cooling, such as sliced oranges sprinkled with cinnamon and orange-blossom water. A bowl of fruit, perhaps fresh figs or grapes, and a slice of melon make one forget, too, the spice and heat of the *lekama.*

Just as a point of interest, one of the basic ingredients for many authentic Moroccan dishes is *'smin,* a whitish, greasy substance made from camel fat. It is used as one might use olive oil or butter in browning meats, etc. This fat looks like old-fashioned white lard and can be bought in any market place but its taste is distinctively "camel."

«««««««« »»»»»»»»

One memorable day in Tetuan, on an early visit to Morocco, a young Arab friend asked a woman friend and me, to dine at his house. It meant our first visit to an Arab home and the drama of the occasion seemed even more weighty to Ahmed than to us. The invitation was made several days in advance and again each day thereafter. Ahmed wanted to be sure we really *understood* his invitation and that we were *really* coming. Moroccans, when possible, are lavish and conscientious hosts and he insisted on escorting us from our hotel door to his, guiding us solicitously through the twisting casbah streets, a hand on an elbow of each of us, as carefully as though we were precious porcelain.

His father was a Moroccan army officer and we knew the home could be considered "upper middle class." It stood in the middle of the casbah, a high white wall facing a street of uneven cobbles, littered with donky dung. Far-spaced street lights cast thin, spotty illumination. Inside, the house was surprisingly spacious and ornate, with a huge central room, roofed by a peaked skylight. We were the only guests and Ahmed functioned as host and male servant. First he begged us to accept the hospitality of his "humble home" and knelt down to remove our shoes. With gentle concern, as if we were ancients creaking in every bone, he guided us to low, velvet-covered divans along the wall, plumping cushions for our heads, testing the air with a wet finger to seek out discomforting drafts. A clap of his hands brought an old crone out of the next room, carrying a tray with hot water, towels and jasmine scent. The woman was squat and fat, her unveiled face wrinkled and toothless. Ahmed explained she was an old country Berber, a servant with the family since he was a child. All evening she complained and grumped at him in Arabic, like any crochety grandmother kept up past her bedtime.

Ahmed first moistened his own hands with jasmine scent and then gently massaged the soles of our feet, urging us in Spanish to "be comfortable." Next, he held out a beaten brass basin, we extended our hands and he poured over them the warm, scented water. Little towels were passed out for drying and Ahmed sprinkled our hands, wrists and faces with jasmine scent. Then he performed the same ritualistic cleansing for himself.

With the perspiration of hospitality beginning to stand forth on his brow, our host now rolled out a heavy, very large brass tray and heaved it onto low, tripod legs in front of our couch. Pillows were arranged on the floor for Ahmed. The old servant brought in the *diffa:* cous-cous with chicken, vegetables and hot sauces and a big salad made from cut-up tomatoes and green peppers, roasted, peeled and sliced.

In true Moroccan fashion, no knives or forks were used and Ahmed showed us the proper way to eat with the two first fingers and thumb of the right hand. We two used our finger towels as napkins but Ahmed ate with such grace, rolling the cous-cous into tiny balls to pop in the mouth, that only the tips of his fingers were soiled. Like a good host, he selected the most succulent portions of the chicken for us, feeding us bits now and then in simple hand-to-mouth fashion. As a Moslem, he would have nothing alcoholic to drink but had thoughtfully provided two bottles of beer each for his guests, while he sipped an orange pop, trade-marked "Atlas Orange" after the Atlas mountain range.

During the evening, Ahmed made elaborate protestations of hospitality on the part of his mother and young wife, secluded upstairs and—according to custom—unable to join the guests. At one point, his father—who had dined earlier—appeared to give us his greetings, a tall, extremely handsome man, bearded and in long white robes and turban. When he left (to play checkers at a local cafe, Ahmed explained), his son told us that his father had been a Spaniard, coming to Morocco with the Spanish army as a very young man. He fell in love with a veiled girl in the market place, became a Moslem, transferred citizenship and joined the Moroccan Army —and *then* married the veiled girl who was now upstairs, withdrawn and silent, while we enjoyed the hospitality of her house and son. All evening, incidentally, though we knew that there were at least two other adults and a number of children in the house, everything was silent. The women respected the fact that a male of the house was entertaining.

For dessert, we were served platters of sliced melon and then the long ritual of mint tea began. The old Berber tidied the room, clanging brass bowls and thumping irritably at pillows, to show that she was a privileged member of the household. Ahmed settled back with a sigh of contentment, lighting himself an after-dinner pipe of hashish. We lounged and chatted for about two hours, sipping tea while Ahmed asked questions about the United States, told us about his life and country and paused every few minutes to ask anxiously, "You happy?" He spoke little English but his Spanish was excellent, so the conversation was animated. Moroccans have wry, off-beat senses of humor and seem eager for the chance to laugh. Ahmed, when the first pressures of hosting were over, became very relaxed and was so funny that, if we hadn't already been half lying down, we might have "collapsed with laughing."

At our hotel door, we thanked him warmly for this very special evening and he beamed with satisfaction, a dim street-light touching his face and catching a glint of gold in his front teeth. His benevolent, satisfied manner suggested strongly that *he* had been the honored party. "We eat together," he said quietly. "*Now* we are friends. Real friends. *Now* you happy?"

«««««««« »»»»»»»»

Though no host could surpass Ahmed for solicitous warmth, I was privileged to share the great generosity of a wealthy landowner at a wedding feast outside Marrakesh. The guest list was long and we had courteously been included as "strangers" in the area. Just outside the village, cooking tents had been set up in a grove of trees and the dining area on the smooth grass was laid out with colorful Berber rugs, pillows and mattresses. No other woman was present. The pre-feast entertainment was dancing and performances on the drums by young male villagers. The *diffa* itself was large scale—from the whole roast lamb to the huge, straw-covered cous-cous', served on trays as big as tables, with coverings like gaudy sombreros. A third course was chicken cooked with dates and onions and a fourth stewed lamb with vegetables. The heat of the day and the amount of food make the other courses fade from memory. This was, naturally, a Moslem celebration, without wedding champagne, but we were served copiously with mint tea and a delicious cooling drink of almond milk.

«««««««« »»»»»»»»

French food and cooking is, of course, very evident still in the cities and bigger villages all over Morocco. Since the French love good food and are such experts in its preparation, they have always imported their preferences and specialties wherever they live for long. In Casablanca, as in Paris, one may find excellent restaurants serving pâtés, good cheeses and fine wines. And one can shop for the same delicacies and trademarks one finds in France, all imported here.

«««««««« »»»»»»»»

Country dining differs very much from city dining, not only because of variations in income, but because of the remoteness of much country living and the primitive mode of housekeeping. Bread baked in an outdoor oven from home-ground flour, a few vegetables, some boiled goat meat is familiar country fare. Camel's milk is nourishing and popular; chickens and sheep are used only for special feasting. The fact that the average Moroccan workingman's annual income is about $175 makes it clear that the *diffa* spreads mentioned here, though familiar to many, are not everyday fare.

«««««««« »»»»»»»»

I remember one sweltering July day when we stopped for a picnic lunch on a remote road some distance outside Casablanca. Above, the sky was a mercilessly hot, cloudless blue, beating back with heat off the fields of ripe wheat. We pulled the car into the roadside shade of a group of gnarled little trees. The shade around us was as cooling as stepping into water.

The branches looked burdened with a strange "animal fruit." Small black goats were climbing these argan trees (a species rare except in Morocco) to eat the tough, small fruit. Goats love this bitter, black argan product and climb to the highest branches to nibble. Neighboring housewives then cull the goat dung to salvage the fruit pits to squeeze for oil used in back-country illumination.

On this blindingly bright day, we watched the nimble goats for some time, unaware that nearby a young shepherd was watching us. Finally, he stepped from behind some rocks and came close to stare. With him was a little girl of about four, dressed in typical Berber-child costume: barefooted, long green satin dress, ragged at the hem and bound at the waist with heavy satin cord. Her hair, curly and disheveled, was bound round with the same type of cord. Her brother, if he was that, wore simple a torn shirt and grubby shorts. Neither said a word but stared at us intently and curiously, as if we were as odd as the climbing goats.

In our picnic basket we had bread, cheese, sausage and soft drinks and we made sandwiches, passing a share to the two children, who accepted them as calmly as if we brought them lunch every day. They ate hungrily but carefully, smiling now, and we shared and shared alike down to the last crumb. Then the boy fumbled in his pants' pocket and brought out three little yellow apples. He handed one each to us and split the third with a sharp rock, giving half to the girl. Obviously, herding the goats far out of sight of any village, those three apples represented their lunch for the day. We had shared. They had shared. It was a pleasant interlude.

I just hope the children didn't wait for us at that spot too often, hoping for sausage and cheese—and carrying four apples. We never passed that way again.

Chapter IV

TANGIER TO TIZNIT

WHETHER FROM camel-back or Cadillac, a tour of the big-name cities of Morocco is necessary to know the country. Contrasts are great. French-built hotels and public buildings are many-storied, super-modern structures, sketched in white blocks on big-city skylines; ancient casbahs huddle in centuries-old shadow and stone; while country villages are often no more than mud-hut clusters, blending their straw and dust architecture against the earth from which they came.

But from Tangier to Tiznit, each of the following towns spells out a part of Morocco, its past and its present.

RABAT is the capital city, the Washington, D.C. of all Morocco. It is a big, bustling metropolis of over 160,000 people, housing many government buildings and also the sprawling green-roofed palace of the King. The center of Rabat is distinguished by broad, French-planned streets, lined frequently with palm trees and a-hum now with motor vehicles and bicycles. This section of the city has a preoccupied, busy quality about it; it suggests the kind of business that comes from administrative detail and filing clerks, a constant rush to and from offices on official (or red-tape) errands.

The town is laid out in three distinct sections—the *medina,* the *mellah,* and the "European" town, but, since Morocco has become independent, the *medina,* or walled native section, and the European section have begun to meld. The crooked old streets and high-walled private houses of the casbah seem as crowded as ever but more and more Moroccans are moving out, to settle themselves in individual houses, small, square-built and pastel, on broad, open streets and surrounded by tiny gardens overburdened with geraniums and bougainvillaea. The new government has created a political aristocracy progressive enough to enjoy the French-planned homes and suburbs.

The *mellah,* or Jewish section, remains much the same as it has for centuries—narrow streets and high-walled houses, almost indistinguishable from the Moslem sections of town, except that here a synagogue replaces the mosque. The name *mellah,* used to describe the Jewish sections of town all over Morocco, comes, incidentally, from the old Arabic word "salt" and dates back to the days when the "salting of heads" was considered a Jewish specialty. Jews were hired to salt down the heads cut from traitors or enemies captured in battle. These pickled trophies were then posted above the gates or walls of a city. The better the salting job, the longer other enemies might be warned off.

The palace of the King, called Dar-el-Makchzen, is contained within private walls but as part of the city of Rabat. The ruler has sixty inherited palaces but this is the favorite and, since the King has become the active, hard-working head of his country, Rabat is the imperial home.

Dar-el-Makchzen, green-roofed and white-plastered, is a maze of many buildings, some Oriental, some modern in style, built and added to at various times. Here huge rooms are paneled in dark woods, with mosaic floors in yellow, blue and green, radiating in intricate patterns. Couches and divans are covered in expensive velvets and brocades, courtyards are fragrant with flowers and alive with the tinkling of fountains. Many of the chambers show Moroccan styling at its complicated and graceful best, with delicate pillars, high fluted archways and arched windows rimming the walls near the high ceilings, letting in delicate patterns of light but keeping the heat of the Moroccan sun off the cool floors. There is not always cohesion in architecture or interior decoration here, but the palace is stunningly palatial.

Within the courtyard walls are smaller "palaces" for the deceased King's two older daughters, his first and second wives and an assortment of relatives, dependents and old retainers. A small schoolhouse for the younger children is part of the palace plant and a college, founded when the King's oldest son, then Crown Prince Moulay Hassan, reached college age, is just outside the vast grounds.

Among the special features of the main palace is an indoor swimming pool, an innovation in Moslem building, constructed when the modern-thinking Mohammed decided, years ago, that he wanted his girl children to learn the sport in aristocratic privacy. The royal stables house some of the most notable horses in the world. There is also a zoo, on the grounds, stocked in part with animals which were once native to Morocco, such as elephants, ostriches, lions, panthers and monkeys.

««««««««« »»»»»»»»»

Moulay Hassan II, who is believed by the Moslems to be a direct descendant of the Prophet Mohammed, is the spiritual as well as the temporal head of his people. Thus, on every Friday, at noontime, he mounts a gray stallion and, protected by a red and gold umbrella held by a running servant, he rides to worship at the white mosque in the palace compound. His ride is watched and cheered by hundreds of worshipful Moslems, crowded within the palace gates.

All over Morocco, at the same moment, the ritual is duplicated by high ranking officials, representing the King, who go with colorful panoply to the local mosque to pray. Though I never saw the King himself on a Holy Day, I have watched the ceremony many times in Tangier and Casablanca. A brilliantly uniformed guard of mounted horsemen line the roadway leading to the mosque, backed by a milling crowd of spectators. The representative of the King is usually driven to within a block of the mosque, where he leaves his car and mounts a horse. Though the deadline is twelve noon, the ceremonial ride always seems to be delayed, for some reason or other, and the gathering takes on a holiday aspect, with soft drink vendors and peanut urchins doing a brisk trade. The King's representative is greeted with a swelling of cheers and the peculiar Arabic *"yoo-yoo-yoo"* sound of adulation which Moroccan women hoot out from under their veils.

«««««««« »»»»»»»»

Rabat takes its name from "Rabat-el-Fath," meaning "Camp of Victory," because it was here that troops assembled at the end of the twelfth century for a planned assault against Spain. Though it is situated on the Atlantic coast and thus benefits both from the sea breezes and the beauty of the background, this town has never been a prosperous, modern port because of an obtruding sand bar across the harbor. However, centuries ago, before the harbor silted over, Rabat was the Atlantic outport for goods arriving by camel train from all over Morocco. Later it became a notorious pirate port, from which the Barbary pirates sailed forth, looting on the high seas as far afield as the English Channel. At one time, says an old history book, a "college for pirates" held regular classes on cutlass know-how right in Rabat!

Two memory pictures that are distinctly "Rabat" are morbidly picturesque: one is the huge graveyard close to the sea, its rectangular headstones serving as a windbreak for part of the city. The other is the tomb of an ancient Moroccan holy man, Sidi Ben Ashir, who worked in his lifetime for a more compassionate treatment of lunatics. Even today, his decorated shrine is visited by those who wish to pray on behalf of mentally disturbed relatives. Occasionally, the relative is brought along on the pilgrimage and the groups make their prayers—and then settle down for a rather strained family picnic nearby.

«««««««««« »»»»»»»»»»

CASABLANCA, which means "white house" in Spanish, is today a great cluster of busy docks, cranes, freighters, splendid office buildings, wide boulevards and crowded, sprawling casbah, clinging along the Atlantic coast and overlooking a superb harbor. Since the days—as recently as forty years ago—when it was only a "white house on a cliff" to guide sailors in from the sea, Casablanca has grown into a prosperous town of 600,000 people.

This is an active, pulsing city, with a feverish history of conquest, capture, build-up and breakdown. Some historians say it was founded by the Phoenicians, others credit the Romans. The Moroccans record that it was first built by Berber tribesmen. In the middle of the fifteenth century, Portuguese colonizers decided to root out this second pirate base and destroyed the whole town. Later, they returned to rebuild it, only to be driven out by earthquakes some three hundred years later. After that came the Spaniards and, in the early 1900's, the French, who have left the print of their planning, ambitions and business enterprise marked clearly over the city.

Casablanca has a number of elegant hotels, tall white buildings offering every luxury in food, lodging and plush-living comfort. It also has some of the world's worst slums, housing thousands in poverty and squalor. Both are direct results of the fact that this is also one of the fastest growing cities on earth. In size, it is number four in all Africa and in tonnage handled at the port, it ranks just above the famous French port of Marseilles.

Place de France, a traffic-burdened circular "square," is the heart of town and from it radiate all the important streets of the city, with the ancient *medina* on one side and the banks, hotels and department stores of present day Casablanca on the other. Within a short walking distance (but watch that humming traffic!), one can shop for such French imports as nylon underclothing, chic bathing suits and hi-fi equipment in modern department stores. Nearby, in the dim bazaars and *souks* one finds hand-woven wool rugs, beaten brass trays, inlaid boxes and leather goods, the handicrafts of the country itself.

As an example of the contrasts in Casablanca, one may look at the Hotel El Mansour, standing in the center of town, as glittering and modern as an upright tray of ice-cubes. The lobby is luxurious with yellow leather and muted violet furniture; a fountain plays with mechanical perfection. Waiters are white-gloved and carefully trained; soft music is piped into the dining room. In the elegant sleeping rooms, there are push buttons for every service from wines to shoeshines. The hotel is open to anyone, Moroccan or foreign—who can afford it.

Yet surrounding the hotel, in any vacant-lot shelter or unguarded doorway, one can find homeless Moroccans, young men and unemployed oldsters, huddled up for a free night's sleep.

«««««««««« »»»»»»»»»»

Outside the town lies a giant slum city of shacks, made mostly from old boards, flattened tin cans and sheet metal roofing. Here, thousands of people are jammed into squalid quarters that bake in heat and dust in the summertime and run with mud and chill in the rains of winter. Casablanca has simply grown too fast to bed down all its residents in anything resembling comfort or health.

A number of years ago, the French began construction on the "new *medina*," a well-laid-out area, resembling a casbah in its privacy and basic construction but with wider streets, more frequent fountains for water and with sunshine, fresh air and greater sanitation as its general aim. All the buildings are painted chalk white and the town has an air of well-scrubbed cleanliness—but even this "new *medina*" is now crowded to overflowing. The Moroccans themselves must continue planning and building, to keep up with a growing Casablanca.

At night, whether viewed from the sea or the inland plains, this city gleams like a paradise, and its gleam is a beacon to the unemployed or glamour-struck youth from the *bled* (countryside). To many farm boys, to grow up means to move to Casablanca.

At one time, there was work for all in this thriving industrial city, with warehouses and elevators storing grains and other products, to be shipped all over the world. There were also breweries, shoe factories, machine shops and flour mills, besides the innumerable smaller craft factories. But when Morocco became independent, much French capital and interest was withdrawn. Unemployment struck hardest in the big cities. Thus Casablanca may still *seem* the mecca for unskilled workers, but for many, the dream proves an empty one; hence the crowded shack slums, the unemployed workers wandering the streets and the numerous sleepy, shelterless men huddled in doorways.

Even with its size and industry, Casablanca—like every major Moroccan city—never seems far from the countryside, and the barefooted Berber women, the donkeys with heavy panniers and the vendors hawking chickens and melons, venture in town as far as the sophisticated *Place de France*. Growth has been steady but sometimes rather haphazard. A modern office building may be adjoined by a rubble-littered lot holding a temporary shack dwelling, a bit of garden and a tethered goat.

Suburban areas, developed and cultivated by the French into luxury living spots, with triple-bath homes and exquisite gardens, now hold many empty and deteriorating houses. When French businessmen withdrew to their native land, the Moroccans chose to overlook these real estate bargains, either because they could not afford them or because they found the French structures, without separate living quarters for the women, etc., unsuited to Moslem living. Or because, as a Moroccan journalist pointed out, there is revenge in refusing to live in the house of the enemy.

«««««««« »»»»»»»»

Even today, prejudices and tempers sometimes flare out in Morocco and memories of past troubles seem much alive.

After many trips, the country seems a familiar and friendly place to me but I remember (and with a smile now) my very acute alarm on a first visit to Casablanca itself, just after independence was granted.

We had driven down from Rabat rather late on a summer evening. On the outskirts of Casablanca a series of traffic policemen began waving us along back-street routes, though our destination—the El Mansour hotel—is in the center of the city. Finally we approached the big structure by a back alley and carried our own bags around to the front door. The main lobby was ringed with an armed guard, an elite group of dark-skinned men, each standing over six feet tall, wearing brilliant red draped coats, green bloused trousers and with sharply curved scimitars hung at the waist. From our fourth floor room, we could look out at the street below, lined at regular intervals along the curb with uniformed policemen. Traffic was nonexistent and over the area hung an ominous, militarily-controlled silence. Was this civil war, and invasion, some new trouble to tear Morocco apart?

Apprehensive, we finally called the room clerk to ask if "anything special is going on."

"Why, yes," was his cheerful answer. "King Mohammed is on the mezzanine at this moment, visiting an art exhibit. The King's Honor Guard is standing in the lobby. Do come down with your cameras. They would make wonderful color slides. . . ."

«««««««« »»»»»»»»

Marrakesh is the "red city" of Morocco, set in the southern plains, above the Sahara area, and with every wall and building aglow with the rose-red shades of the surrounding clay. Where Casablanca gleams white, Marrakesh blushes a becoming sand-red, as if "overcome by its own beauty."

This city of nearly 200,000 people is more than 900 years old. It is ringed on three sides by the high, snow-covered Atlas Mountains whose waters irrigate the plain till Marrakesh blooms like a rare desert flower. The Atlas ranges reach to 12,000 feet at certain peaks and, even in the bake of summer, its snows cool the atmosphere of Marrakesh, give it an incomparably beautiful background and provide, through intricate underground wells and piping, the precious water that keeps this city alive and a-bloom.

To rave about the beauties of Marrakesh is just reflex action after seeing the city. Thousands have done this, from weary caravaneers to Sir Winston Churchill, who has made it his favorite painting spot for years.

Marrakesh is half surrounded by a 32,000-acre park of palm trees—over 90,000 in all—which give a prelude of coolness and grace to the town itself, part of which is still surmounted by centuries-old red walls. The in-town streets are lined with bitter-orange trees, fragrant with blossom in spring and summer and dotted with gold all winter long. Fountains and gardens are brightened with jasmine, bougainvillaea, almond trees and other brilliant tropical flowers. Many of the main thoroughfares are lined with tall jacaranda trees, heavy with lavender blossoms.

This town was founded by desert tribes who, under a strong leader, settled on this spot to cease their wanderings. Even today, Marrakesh has a strong Saharan-African flavor, with darker skins and an air of individuality in its people. Much of the "darker blood" came to Marrakesh through slaves and, until the time of the French protectorate, or until about forty-five years ago, it was an important slave center, with public auctions held in the market place three times a week.

In the days of these markets, slaves were of two classes:

dark-skinned "fresh slaves," imported from below the Sahara, and "used" slaves, those confiscated from a wealthy household that had fallen into disfavor with the reigning sultan. As the usual procedure, the market place was water-sprinkled to hold down dust, prayers were offered to Allah, and wealthy buyers arranged themselves comfortably, lighting pipes and chatting as at a social gathering. Slaves—men, women and children—were paraded around the market place, while an auctioneer took bids and decided prices. No one was mistreated, shackled or given the physical fetters of slavery; the Koran specifically forbids cruelty to slaves. Buying a child slave as a playmate for a wealthy Moroccan youngster was common practice and over the many, many years that total human output of the sub-Sahara has been absorbed into the Moroccan population.

«««««««« »»»»»»»»

Though it is no longer the political or commercial center it once was, Marrakesh today is the favorite resort city of all Morocco, long the chic Christmas hideaway for the elegant and well-heeled French. It has luxury hotels, a good golf course and excellent December to May skiing in the mountains just a few miles from town.

When the French protectorate was at its profitable height, visitors flocked to the Mamounia Hotel, a converted palace that has lost little of its grandeur by opening its rooms to the paying public. At Christmas time, in those past days, waiters and special foods were flown down from Vichy in France, to make French Christmas in Marrakesh "just like home," though with sunshine, orange trees and an array of soft-footed Berber servants.

The Mamounia is still half-surrounded by the original

palace gardens, intricately flower-patterned, alive with song birds and then "calmed" by an artistic planting of tall palms, which add both shade and peace and seem to absorb all sounds except those which are pleasing—birds, fountains and the murmur of breezes. Great-ceilinged rooms open out to balconies overlooking the gardens; wall-long closets are deep and spacious, designed for ball gowns and many changes of costume; bathrooms are marbled and deep-tubbed, with numbers of bells for summoning servants. As a palace, what luxury was provided for the pashas! As a hotel, what luxury for the French! Today's tourist seems only a spectator at a fast-fading scene.

«««««««« »»»»»»»»

Center city Marrakesh, the French section, is as lined with sidewalk cafes, good resturants and fine shops as any city in France. But it is *old* Marrakesh, the city of the Moroccans, that demands attention.

The *souks* or market places of this town are among the most pleasant of all Morocco. Here, in enlargement, are all the merchandising features of all big-city *souks*. The streets of the casbah are cobbled and winding, but not as narrow as most. In the summertime, these thoroughfares are roofed over, building to building, with slatted cane blinds which blot out the sun and cut the pavement into rythmic light-and-dark patterns. The booths and workmen's shops are bigger here, more active and somehow more artistic. In one, a metal worker may pound his chisel with sharp, ringing strokes as he marks designs into copper. In another, one sees a woodworker, seated on the floor, using a fine saw with both hands while he holds the wood between his feet, toes dexterous as hands.

The dyers' *souk,* where wool is dyed for robes, rugs and bed spreads, is as colorful as a rainbow gone violent. Vast vats of dye bubble and soak with wool, the colors ranging from intense green to reds, blues, yellows and finite black. Above the streets, and often dripping onto the cobblestones, hang drying skeins of wool, like colorful Spanish moss. And everywhere clings the acrid, wet-ink smell of dyes. The colors, the patterns of hanging wool are stunning in their brilliance. The mood of this *souk* is one of subdued but obvious good humor. Why? Because it is almost impossible not to react, to smile and feel gay among such an extravagance of color.

For centuries, Marrakesh has been famous for its square in the heart of the city called *Djema El Fna* or "the meeting place of the dead." In decades past, public executions were held here and the heads of the victims, plus decapitated trophies of rebels killed in battle (or the head of anyone who had radically displeased a sultan) were nailed to the walls. Where people once came to stare at these horrible symbols of power, they now come to shop and, above all, to be entertained.

By day, in the blistering sunlight, merchants sell vegetables and fruits. Food is everywhere, for taking home or eating on the spot. A favorite of this market place is a porridgelike gruel called *el ben,* served with milk in a small bowl. Hot doughnut-type cakes are cooked in deep fat, sending an oily fragrance over the square. Female basket weavers work and sell on the spot and used-goods merchants set up shop simply by arranging a collection of saleable debris around them, everything from worn tires to Wesson Oil cans and old clothing, some still sporting Fifth Avenue labels.

Both barbers and dentists establish open-air trade in *Djema El Fna* by arranging a chair under a sloping wicker shade. Beards are clipped, heads trimmed and the hair is swept into the gutters with a twig broom. Frequently, economy-minded farmers buy the "once-over-lightly" treatment, allowing the barber to shave off all face and head hair for a few cents.

Dentists, operating without the benefit of sanitation or anesthetic, are chiefly involved in extractions. Each dentist displays a box of pulled teeth as an advertisement of his skill and experience.

Both barbers and "doctors" practice the art of bloodletting, still much favored in Morocco as a cure for headaches and a number of other ailments. A small cut is lanced on the nape of the neck, a tiny metal pipe applied and the blood sucked out by the practitioner, to be deposited in a little bowl. Sometimes this public barbaring and bloodletting makes one feel that the beheading of past decades is still going on!

Other "doctors" or medicine men staff booths which sell such healing ingredients as dried adder puffs, foxes' teeth, dried mice and locusts and old standbys like cats' tails and monkeys' paws. The liver of the jackal ("he who never sleeps") is considered a good wake-up aid for night watchmen or people starting on long journeys, and the saliva of foxes is a love potion most potent. These sorcerer-doctors have an ingredient or combination for any ailment, some superstitious, some valid. For the simple headache, for instance, a simple remedy; a light massage along the muscles at the back of the neck.

In the late afternoon, the *Djema El Fna* comes alive as a place of entertainment, hopping with people who seem, in their multitudes, to become as microscopic and jumpy as trained fleas. The performers simply wait to draw a crowd and begin a show any time they are suitably ringed with spectators. Some groups act out simple playlets, changing costumes and characters by switching hats, shawls, picking up a dagger, etc. Tumblers and acrobatic troupes are popular, usually itinerate young men who play one-week stands at Marrakesh, country villages or seasonal fairs. Boy dancers, accompanied by drums and primitive string instruments, add to the rhythms of the market place.

Favorite performers at *Djeme El Fna,* and in most festive market places all over the country, are the snake-charmers, oddly violent looking fellows whose long, ropy hair is their trademark. Some snake charmers carry their performing reptiles coiled up on a little pillow; others seem to travel with a "team," toting a collection of snakes in a straw basket, slung around the neck like a fishing creel.

In a performance, the serpents are allowed to coil and twist about the neck and arms of the charmer, or the performer plays a little flute while the snake gyrates upwards, from the ground, responding to the music as if he were reaching for a high note. Some of the reptiles are presumably adders, (I couldn't honestly distinguish a python from a garden hose) rendered temporarily less dangerous. Before a performance, they are "teased" with a folded cloth until they strike again and again, drying up the poisonous fluid in the fangs. Garter snakes are frequently used and, after a suitable amount of entertainment, i.e. prodding, twisting and gyrating the reptile, many performers make a dramatic *finale* by biting off the snake's head!

I watched one snake charmer off and on through a whole evening. At the end of each performance, he held his reptile close to his face as the creature presumably struck, bringing blood to his nose and gasps from the crowd. But even Moroccan show business has its little secrets; just before one performance I spotted the charmer off in a corner, gently loosening a scab on his nose, to get it ready for the big, "bloody," crowd-shocking windup to his act.

Comedians and storytellers always draw crowds. In a country where so many persons cannot read or write, it is often the storytellers who pass down the history of the lands, recounting the valiant deeds of long-dead pashas and warriors. (In fact, in the recent struggle for independence, many "storytellers" roused their audiences with strong anti-French propaganda and the French temporarily closed *Djema El Fna* to all gatherings.) Moroccan market place comedians reel off a repertoire like any ancient court jester or current TV comedian who knows from experience what makes people laugh. Many times, the jokes are old ones, pleasing for their familiarity as well as their humor.

Here is an "old joke," translated for me, which I believe is funny in any language:

"A poor young Moslem, much down on his luck, was traveling through the countryside, looking for work—and for food, water and lodging. In his travels, he came upon a saint's shrine, where lived a holy man, or *marabout,* a well-fed, luxuriously clothed ancient who made a good living by collecting fees from those who wanted to pray at the saint's shrine.

"To this old holy man, the young traveler came, begging help. Taking pity, the *marabout* fed him, gave him a donkey and sent him on his way across the sands. A short distance on, the donkey sickened in the intense heat and died. The young man buried the donkey, heaping stones above his body in an intricate pattern until he had a "shrine." A short time later, a second traveler appeared, was told that a saint was buried in the shrine—and paid alms to be allowed to pray.

"Before long, business became so good that streams of pilgrims came to the donkey's grave, praying, giving alms and making the young man rich. One day the old *marabout* arrived, to find out what had been siphoning off his business.

"His protege confessed. 'Yes, O Father, I have no saint in my shrine. Only the body of the poor donkey you gave me. But tell me, pray, what saint is buried in your sacred shine?'

" 'O, young man,' the marabout replied, rolling his eyes to heaven. 'Our saints are related. For in my shrine lies the *mother* of your donkey.' "

«««««««« »»»»»»»»

Other storytellers are more philosophical, choosing the kind of grain-of-truth tales that have made folk stories and fables lasting in all countries. And a good storyteller is also a good actor, dramatizing his lines, changing voice for different characters and holding his audience at attention for an hour or more. An Arab friend told me this tale which has been a spellbinder in the market places for decades and is known to almost every child in Morocco. It is called "the story of the unfinished slippers" and goes this way:

An old but wealthy man had a favorite wife, a young and lovely girl named Jasmina. Sometimes her beauty was such a challenge to him that he felt angry with her and one day, in a fit of temper, he shouted out three times the severing words, "I divorce you!" Instantly, he was filled with regret but, being a good Moslem, he had to abide by Koranic law, i.e., a man must not remarry his divorced wife until she has been the bride of another man.

Wandering then through the market place, he spied a young and impoverished shoemaker at work on a pair of delicate green slippers. "Will you do something for me with a bag of gold as payment?" the wealthy man asked. The young shoemaker nodded.

"You will marry a lady of my harem," the old man directed. "You will be her husband for just twenty-four hours and then you will divorce her. For this I will pay you a bag of gold. Do I have your promise?"

"I will divorce her as soon as I have finished these slippers in my hand," said the shoemaker. "You have my promise."

So the lovely young Jasmina and the handsome shoemaker were married and twenty-four hours later the wealthy man came to the shoemaker's booth, carrying a bag of gold. But, to his dismay, he saw the young man tapping away on a pair of red slippers. Behind him, on a peg, hung the green slippers, unfinished. The older man left with a sigh and a heavy heart. Young love had conquered. The shoemaker had broken no promise—and the green slippers would never be finished in his lifetime."

Depending on the mood of the audience, either tale will hold a crowd in the *Djema El Fna,* any night just before the sun goes down.

«««««««« »»»»»»»»

FEZ is an ancient and picturesque city, about 100 miles inland from both the Mediterranean and the Atlantic Ocean, the artistic and educational heart of all Morocco. It is, in fact, two towns—the old city, dating back well over a thousand years, and the new city, built by the French in the 1900's and housing French residential and government districts, plus a special area for Jews. The old Fez stretches between low hills in the valley of a broad river and is surrounded by groves of orange, pomegranate and other fruit trees, as well as the silver-green of olive groves. It has a drainage system superior to most Moroccan towns and is, therefore, curiously cleaned. Periodically, drains are opened to flood the streets and all dust and refuse is washed away. This thorough but medieval type of sanitation is typical of the "old world" life and mood of the whole town.

The name Fez (or Fas) means "pickax." A combination of history and legend records that, in 808 A.D., Moulay Idriss II, a religionist and scholar, and son of the man who brought the faith of Islam to Morocco, broke the first ground for this city with a golden pickax. His "ground breaking speech" went this way: "I have come to build a town where I will live, where my children will live, and, after me, where his highness God will be adored, his book read and his laws and religion will be followed." From that day, the town grew and prospered, reaching cultural peaks and existing at one time as the most famous town in the North of Africa.

Today, it is a city with a hundred mosques and, supposedly, one thousand palaces, all clustered together along shadowy, narrow streets, broken here and there with a fountain-centered square and lush gardens. Old Fez has not a single European building and its walls, arched gates and complicated interior decorations are as extravagant and breathtaking as a dream from the *Arabian Nights*. Cedar beams and good stone have been used in much of the building, hence Fez does not have the crumbling look so common to Moroccan cities.

In the center of town, the *Karueein mosque* is famous as the largest mosque in Africa. Its main low-roofed structure is supported by 366 pillars, with an adjoining chapel for services for the dead held up by 24 rhythmic pillars, all bearing horseshoe arches. Inside, the mosque is lit by over 1700 lights. So sacred a shrine is this structure, built by the founder of the city just two years after the first stroke of the gold pickax, that special rules are imposed on all nonbelievers; in short, the streets to its entrance are forbidden to Jews, Christians and four-footed beasts.

The *medina* and *souks* radiate out from the great mosque into narrow but graceful streets, covered in summer by the matting roofs. Fez is very cold in the wintertime but the heat of the summer is intense. Again, as in most *souks,* different streets are devoted to different merchants or craftsmen but the *souks* of Fez have special emphasis. Here, because it is a religious town, one finds the streets of the sellers of incense and candles. Then come the streets of booksellers, stationers and binders, because it is a university town; and the streets of weavers and cloth dealers, because the middle class of Fez are chiefly clothing merchants. Next are ranged the streets of the silversmiths, glassblowers and pottery makers, since Fez for nearly a thousand years has been famous for the skill of its craftsmen. Along with their other skills, Fez merchants are acclaimed for their shrewdness and honesty.

This is a scholars' town, with the University of Fez and a number of surrounding *medersas,* or colleges. Students are a familiar sight, usually rather thin, solemn-faced young men, loaded down with books. In the earliest days of Islam, Fez was famous for its schools of religion, philosophy and astronomy. After the Moors were expelled from Spain, many fled to Fez, bringing new information on the arts, sciences and manufacturing from the Spanish world. (That influx of "new knowledge" came, however, about 500 years ago!) Today, the town draws students from all over Morocco, Algeria and Tunisia, as well as lower Africa. Religion, philosophy and the arts are still the major studies but, more and more, the colleges are trying to introduce subjects which will help the students to give more modern service to their world: engineering, agriculture and the industrial sciences. It is not infrequent now to see in Fez a door plaque reading: "Ahmed Hantout, Lawyer. Sorbonne, Paris," or some such indication that more "new knowledge" is flowing into Fez.

To be a student in Fez means simply to study. There is no campus life, no dating and no sports, except a spontaneous game of soccer played in a near-town field. (It is amusing to watch the students in a heated game, long *djellabas* flapping and heelless slippers staying in place even when kicking the ball.) Students can live at the colleges, paying no fees but possessing a key to a sleeping room, a key which is bought and paid for by one student, then sold to his successor. The rooms are simple—straw matting, a *burnoose* (blanket-type covering) and equipment to make mint tea. Most students are very poor and the townspeople consider it an honor and an obligation to feed one now and then. A merchant may subsidize a student for a few weeks of food or invite him to his home for an intellectual evening and a stomach-filling meal of cous-cous and tea.

There is in Fez a medieval feeling, an atmosphere of withdrawn scholarship about the colleges and the students; yet it was among the intellectuals of Fez that the first feeling of Moroccan nationalism came alive more than thirty years ago. These religious-philosophical students *can* see beyond the rims of their ancient books and over the walls of the old town.

Fez seems to hold the essence of all that is historically or artistically important in Morocco; its physical containment, the narrow streets, intricate arches, tilings and fountains, the fragrances of its orchards and the scent of its spices all give it a secret, endless quality. Few travelers have ever visited Fez and claimed to understand it—or to have truly seen more than a glimpse of its great beauty.

Moroccans themselves are overawed by this city. As one eighteenth century poet explained:

"This garden-girt city
Is like the face of a handsome youth framed in blooming down.
Its *wadi* (canals) are like the bent forearm of a beautiful woman
And the firmly wrought bridges are her bracelets."

«««««««« »»»»»»»»

TIZNIT is an oasis town, far south in Morocco, on the edge of the Sahara and surrounded by arid desolation. It is a garden spot servicing miles of sun-baked, flat sand lands, grubbed over only by sparse, dry growths of cactus.

After Marrakesh and Agadir, one passes the last of the straw-topped Berber villages and the rare twisted groves of juniper trees. As one travels down, down, near to the heat and sand, the land flattens and dries, the people become darker, rougher and more colorful in appearance. Suddenly, against the horizon, loom the high, serrated walls of Tiznit. Today, the town can be approached by private car, donkey or by jostling, crowded autobuses. Over hundreds of years in the past, it was a welcome sight to camel caravans, trekking down to start the long journey across the Sahara. Even today, a weathered road marker stands outside the gates of Tiznit, pointing farther south and marked, simply: TIMBUKTU. This is the south of Morocco—hot, dusty and different.

About 7,000 people live within the ancient walls of Tiznit in a town divided into four quarters, for the four separate Berber tribes which make up most of the population. And there is a special *mellah* for the less than 500 Semites who have chosen to serve out their lives in this dusty isolation. Today, with coastal freighters and airplanes replacing most of the old camel traffic to lower Africa, Tiznit exists chiefly as a market town for the surrounding *bled.* Its central square of sun-baked clay, as big as a football field, sees a daily coming and going of ramshackle busses, loaded to the running boards with everything from passengers to live chickens and camel saddles. And the same square is lined with hitching posts for lordly camels, and small donkeys, restless and braying in the sun.

Inside the walls, graceful date palms cast slight shadows and, at the height of noon, everything human seeks shelter from the sun inside the flat-topped houses. Most of these homes are two-story, red clay structures, with tiny windows and exterior staircases and with walled-in gardens to protect tiny plantings of vegetables and green stuffs. The family goat, valuable for both its meat and milk, is usually tethered just out of reach of the vegetation.

In the *souk* section of town, the streets are a hive of activity, with the eager merchants selling every desert-country need from water bags to camel bells. Tiznit is the jewelry-making center of Southern Morocco and the silversmiths and other craftsmen sit in their dim shops amid a confusion of chains, brooches, thick silver ankle bracelets and stone-laden "hands of Fatima." The latter pieces of jewelry, literally hand-shaped, are considered good-luck symbols. They are supposed to solicit the protection of Fatima, daughter of the Prophet Mohammed. Many are expensive. Some are worn as earrings, others as bracelet charms, while a large favorite, bigger than a life-size hand, is worn on a chain around the female neck, protecting—it would seem—the whole chest.

The women of the south differ from their northern sisters in some ways. Mostly they are hard-working, good-looking women, outgoing and decorative and yet, in the southern countryside, we encountered more "shy" Moslem women than nearer the cities. These latter not only cover themselves in the usual all-over drapings of white, with face veil, they also add extra layers of yellow and red and white striped cloth, even pulling a tail of these garments *over the face veil* when passing males or strangers!

The true Berber farm woman in this area is more free and often wears the total costume mentioned above but with both face and arms completely uncovered. Intricate metal and chain headdresses, like heavy iron crowns dangling with medals, sit just above the hairline, while wrists, ankles and fingers are a-clank with jewelry. In some cases, the heat of the south brings out behavior which is certainly radical for Moslem women: the famous women *guedra* dancers of this area perform not only publicly but with faces exposed and low-cut necklines. In short, this is the Saharan south—closer in appearance and habit to what we have long thought of as "Africa."

The "sacred waters" of this oasis town are a curiously shallow pool, about sixty feet by sixty, surrounded by steep rock sides and fed by underground springs. Its sacredness, nevertheless, does not keep the townspeople from putting it to practical use. Cows clump gracelessly down to drink, children scoop up bucketsful of the water, to carry home, and groups of women kneel on the banks, scrubbing clothes in the tepid pond. The whole sluggish green surface, lit by the sun, is shot through with tiny minnows. Near the pond rises the mosque of Tiznit, its towers marked by clusters of queer, protruding poles, believed to be "roosts for the dead."

Small, dry and dusty as it may seem to strangers, Tiznit is the big-city glamour spot for miles of desolate countryside all around. It is the social and entertainment capital. Here dancers gather to perform in the square, while storytellers and musicians try to find a shady spot to draw an audience.

The people one sees are "Moroccan cosmopolitan," including black-skinned Sudanese, up from below in the desert, and the "blue men," those distinctively tinted citizens of Goulamine whose skin is permanently blued from decades of wearing cheap blue-dyed cloth. Common visitors to town are the mountain Berber men, mostly wearing rough-woven black coats, with a small, round red-and-yellow marking between the shoulder-blades, a good luck omen to ward off the "evil eye." Fascinating, too, is the occasional "veiled man," a Moroccan observing the tradition of his conservative tribe which even veils its males.

After sundown, the town goes quiet with a small-town silence, with perhaps a few men lingering around a single light bulb in a café or a storyteller spinning out a last yarn beside a guttering ramekin of lighting oil. At night, the *fondouks,* or inns, are crowded with travelers and their beasts; these *fondouks* are "hotel-stables," where donkeys and camels bed down with their masters, sharing the same straw as mattresses and warming each other on chill nights. A male friend of mine, short on funds, spent a night in one of the *fondouks.* (They are forbidden to women.) It happened to be a late fall evening and the floor fluttered with drafts. While other weary journeyers slept close to the warmth of their animals, my friend tossed and turned uncomfortably. Finally, an Arab near the doorway tiptoed outside and came back with a smile—and a disgruntled but warmly wooly sheep which was lent to my friend for the night!

Its roughness, remoteness and decisively desert character make Tiznit—and the few oasis-fort towns like it—seem much different from such spots as Fez or Rabat. Yet the "oneness" of Morocco, the unity of its current leadership and its educational drives, were made clear again in Tiznit.

On the back wall of the city, near a battered gate letting

out from a slum area, was displayed a huge colored poster, cracking and drying in the sun. It showed the King, with arms outstretched, hovering over a little schoolhouse. Into the school door flocked droves of children in the country-cousin dress of the southern area. There was the message printed in Arabic, promising that Mohammed will soon provide education for all Morocco.

Some day soon, even the children of Tiznit will be able to read that message.

«««««««« »»»»»»»»

TANGIER sits high on the Atlantic Coast, just a short channel distance from the famous rock of Gibraltar and the mainland of Spain. It is a spectacular city, perched on this farthest tip of Morocco like a visiting celebrity, part of Africa but resembling Paris or even New York. The distance between southern Tiznit and northern Tangier is great in more than miles.

Until 1956, Tangier was an international city, restored to Morocco only when that country became independent. Right after World War II, it was reputed to be a smuggling center, handling everything from guns to gold. Now it has calmed down and is a reputable, hard-working tourist town, luring travelers with its superb beaches, hotels, night clubs and big gambling casino.

We make a prolonged visit to present-day Tangier in another chapter, so let's look briefly into the city's past. Situated as it is, on the last promontory of the Atlantic Ocean, Tangier is the gateway to the Mediterranean and hence has always been politically important. Legend says that once Spain was joined to Africa at this point and Hercules himself broke apart the narrow band of earth, thus connecting the two

Courtesy French Cultural Services

Morocco, predominantly an agricultural country, boasts rich valley lands but for centuries mountain slopes were unproductive, eroded by wind and weather. French planning introduced extensive electrification programs, scientific irrigation and storage and contour farming.

Courtesy French Embassy Press & Information Division

Casablanca, a teeming port city of 600,000 people, was troubled by over-crowding, plagued by unsanitary, disease-ridden slums. French builders planned this "new *medina*" in the suburbs, using traditional Moroccan designs, but adding sanitation, space and comfort.

Courtesy French Embassy Press & Information Division

Ambitious irrigation program will someday bring water for farming and home use to even most remote spots in Morocco. Today, many primitive villages are still serviced by a single well, with water drawn up by waterwheel and camel power. Same system has existed for many centuries.

Courtesy French Embassy Press & Information Division

Mobile medical units bring modern medicine and hope far into the *bled*.

Moslem mothers seek help in the fight against tuberculosis, eye diseases.

Courtesy French Embassy Press & Information Division

Courtesy French Embassy Press & Information Division

Independence brought thirst for education, fight against 75 per cent illiteracy.

Here is a fortunate class; some schools must crowd seventy students in one room.

Courtesy French Embassy Press & Information Division

Courtesy Moroccan Chamber of Commerce

Since the fabled days of the Barbary pirates, Morocco's long coast lines have furnished good ports for commercial and fishing vessels. Ships of all nations pick up outgoing cargoes of Moroccan minerals, citrus fruits, cereals and cork. White-domed building in foreground is saint's shrine.

Courtesy Moroccan Chamber of Commerce

Goats forage for fruit of argan tree; fruit pits are squeezed for lamp oil.

Courtesy Moroccan Chamber of Commerce

Chief mountain range is the Atlas, with many peaks perpetually snow-capped.

Courtesy Moroccan Chamber of Commerce

Tiznit is an oasis town, surrounded by high brown walls and built around a sacred pool. Jewelry-manufacturing center for the south, it is an active, commercial area, served by both rickety buses and camel traffic. Mosque in background shows protruding poles, built for dead souls to "roost."

Courtesy Moroccan Chamber of Commerce

The brilliance of orange trees against red clay walls, the fragrance of jasmine and lilies, the distant shine of snow on blue mountains—this is Marrakesh. A garden city fed by mountain rivers, it is the center of "Red Morocco." Visitors from all over admire this beauty spot.

Courtesy Moroccan Chamber of Commerce

Each dusk, the cooling air smells of hot-fat doughnuts, donkeys and fresh melons. Storytellers chant out ancient tales; dancers and musicians perform before applauding circles; snake charmers thrill the crowd with fang-mouthed serpents. This is Djema-Fna-Place, the market heart of Marrakesh.

Courtesy Moroccan Chamber of Commerce

Moroccans are skilled handicraftsmen. Behind such doors are homes with carved ceilings, intricately tiled floors and lanterns cut to give patterned light; beauty behind high walls, huddled close on narrow streets.

Courtesy Moroccan Chamber of Commerce

Delicate handicraft work marks Moroccan architecture. This palace shows arches with spun-sugar workmanship, in courtyard designed to enhance both sunlight and shadow. But only the very wealthy enjoy such home beauties as these.

In this land of contrasts, modern cities such as Port Lyautey are never far from primitive country villages. Most big towns are distinctly divided between the Moroccan-planned *medinas* and the wide-street skyscraper towns built by the French, "little Parises" set down on foreign soil.

Courtesy Moroccan Chamber of Commerce

Courtesy Moroccan Chamber of Commerce

A moroccan garden must have three things: running water, cool shadows and flower scents. Most city homes are built around open courtyard, planted as garden, used as sitting room, play area or sunny spot to dry family wash.

Courtesy Moroccan Chamber of Commerce

Annual Feast of the Sheep is a day of prayer and rejoicing. Here crowd waits before mosque for word that the sacrificial mutton has met "blessed death."

Courtesy Moroccan Chamber of Commerce

Every Friday, the Moslem holy day, the King rides ceremoniously to near-by mosque for noon-time prayers. In each major town, King's representatives, splendidly garbed, make similar trips to offer prayers to Allah.

seas. The "caves of Hercules" are an important landmark of Tangier, deep, wave-washed openings in the rock, half natural and half artificial, since centuries of Moroccan hewers have cut their millstones out of these caves.

At various times, starting some 1600 years ago, this fine port city has been in the hands of the Phoenicians, Carthaginians and Romans. Later came the Portuguese and the Spanish. Then, for about thirty-five years, until 1956, Tangier was an international port, governed by a committee of representatives of the United States, Belgium, France, Great Britain, Holland, Italy, Portugal and Spain.

Though this proud city is now part of the domain of Hassan II, it is still firmly and profitably in the hands of the tourists.

Chapter V

CAMELS, CADILLACS—AND CASBAHS

RAILROADS AND transport trucks carry much of the heavy goods of this nation, taxis screech through the city streets and even an occasional Cadillac may gleam on a main highway, but the big brown camel is still the transportation and burden-bearing king of Morocco. It is the camel that serves the farmer, links village to village and country to town and decorates the landscape with the familiar, contradictory, gawky grace of the humped body. In the countryside, this beast identifies the horizon like a trademark.

Camels, sturdy and enduring, can pull a plow, turn a water wheel, carry two men or more or haul a burden of straw, wood, or farm produce weighing up to 500 pounds. This is a special animal, first used as a work beast more than 3,000 years ago and well adapted to sand, heat and desert climates. Its nostrils can close as tightly as its mouth to keep out sand; a special transparent eyelid slides over the eyeball in dust storms. Wide, soft feet are made to spread out flatly, giving a walking grip on shifting sands. Camel meat and camel milk supplement country diets and nomad tribes know that camel urine is a protection against sunburn. Hair from the camel, bristling and strong, makes excellent cloth for tenting and the hide can be tanned down into the softest leather for hassocks, bags and heelless slippers. The beast needs little to sustain it, eating chiefly leaves and grasses, and it can survive for days without food or water, a helpful, strong-backed companion to man, who has been made more weak and prone to thirst.

Most major villages hold a "camel market" once a week, for the purchase or trading of these work beasts. The camels are tethered to low stacks in a central clearing, usually lying down with their knobby legs folded under them, staring about in a crochety, old-man fashion and emitting frequent complaining brays that display their thick, vibrating gray tongues.

Male camels, in the mating season, are known to be wickedly bad-tempered, wont to fight with other males and gurgling in their throat with a coarse, bubbly sound that suggests indigestion more strongly than a love call. Also, in this season, the males blow out a strange, sticky substance that looks and smells like malodorous bubble gum. Once, in a Berlin zoo, I was spat at rather savagely by a love-struck camel but those I saw in Morocco seemed remarkably passive.

Young camels have the same wizened, unfinished look that often characterizes baby birds and thus resemble diminutive but aged replicas of their mothers, with scruffy hides, rickety legs and wrinkled brows. These young beasts are suckled for a year and do not reach maturity until they are sixteen or seventeen. A healthy beast will live to be forty or fifty, thus bearing its burdens and serving its master for thirty years or more. To buy a new camel is a serious, long-range investment and the camel markets are places for considered comparing, examining and bargaining.

Besides carrying loads of all sorts, the camel is indispensable in turning the rural water wheels, to fill irrigation ditches and village reservoirs. Huge wooden wheels, equipped with white clay cups for scooping up water, are turned round and round, to raise water from deep wells. In the sun-bright country stillness, it is a peaceful sight to see one of these faithful beasts, usually blindered against distractions, winding its eternal circle around a well, the soft plod of its feet and the tinkle of water the only sounds in a quiet day. Its master may plow a field miles away, trek off to market or nap in the shade of his hut, but the one-humped dromedary works on and on, never breaking stride until untethered and led away for the night.

Occasionally, an entire village is served by one camel, housed in a water-house constructed over the well. I remember one such water-house with its camel installed on the second floor, treading out his life in a twelve-by-twelve space. This dromedary was blindered with woven-straw blinkers that looked like "desert ear-muffs," and the floor was sanded to make his padded feet more comfortable. In an adjoining room, the camel was bedded down each night on a heap of straw. The same beast had worked the wheel for ten years without a day off. How many times he might have made the desert trek to Timbuktu and back—if he had been walking a straight path.

Camels, say myth-minded Moroccans, walk with head held tall and high because they are proud beasts, proud of the fact that they are the "only living things that know the hundredth name of God." I, too, became very sentimentally fond of Moroccan camels. They are exciting to look at—and seemed to be hard-working, loyal and affectionate. Then, to my surprise and information, I read this statement by British camel-authority, Sir F. Palgrave: "He (the camel) is from first to last an undomesticated and savage animal rendered serviceable by stupidity alone, without much skill on his master's part, or any cooperation on his own save that of an extreme passiveness. Neither attachment nor even habit impress him; never tame, though not wide-awake enough to be exactly wild."

«««««««« »»»»»»»»

If camels are the "animal trademark" of this country, then storks are the bird symbol. These huge birds, black and white with red legs and beaks, are considered to bring good luck and are accorded honored treatment wherever they choose to roost. "Father Red Legs," as Moroccans call the bird, is calm and confident, never fluttering off at the approach of humans and even sitting serenely on flat-topped roofs when the women of the house come up for sun and air. Each straw-topped Berber country hut is trimmed with a final crown of rough-stick nesting in which sits a big stork. And I can remember the sunset loveliness of the town of Taouradant with its high, red serrated walls, a stork nesting between each notch, silhouetted against a flaming sky. No Moroccan child would dream of throwing stones or otherwise molesting a stork or its eggs. An injured bird or a baby fallen from the nest is piously nursed back to health, for the stork is sacred to the Moroccans.

An old legend says that, centuries ago, an arrogant sultan laughed at a group of poor but devout pilgrims who had journeyed to a saint's shrine. In anger, Allah turned the sultan into a stork, and ever since the Sultan's descendants have been trying to make amends, roosting close and bringing luck to Moslems only, ignoring the roof-tops of Jews and Christians.

If storks *do* bring luck, then the wealthy of Morocco must be very fortunate indeed. On a poor man's hut, roosts only one bird, while a wealthy house, with many walls and roof peaks, can insure its owner a dozen luck birds.

In the early dusk, the usual period for birds all over the world to fuss and flutter before nest-time, the Moroccan countryside is a-swoop with chattering storks who beat their beaks together in a brittle cacaphony, like rhythmless castanets. It's a delightful sight and sound.

«««««««« »»»»»»»»

All about North Africa, in the countries influenced by the sands and droughts of the Sahara, water is of prime importance. Even in the cities, now plentifully supplied through reservoirs and underground piping, Moroccans retain a racial memory of what water meant in the old years. Each home (except, of course, impoverished dwellings) uses water—and its sound—as a decoration and to add a feeling of luxurious well-being. Behind high walls, one will always find a courtyard garden, floored and tiled in colorful patterns and set about with potted plants, ferns and flowers. And an important part of that courtyard is a fountain, even if it consists of only a single, pencil-thick spout shooting out of a rough clay basin.

In garden planning, Moroccans like to use their water more than once, relishing every gurgle and trickle. For instance, a spray may shoot from the center of a basin, and, as that basin fills, the water tinkles over the edge into a lower floor-set basin with tiny outlets built between the tiles. This water may then trickle off in four or more directions, with each runlet ending in a group of potted plants to which it gives moisture. In intricate formal gardens, fountains may be set high in the center, to give off white-thin sprays or they are even arranged at the top of tile "stairs," so the liquid can run downwards with the burbling music of a contrived waterfall.

Many poorer in-town homes, of course, do not have any running water—even for household uses—and the mistress must then trek several times a day to the nearest public fountain, usually a single water-pipe shooting out into a deep stone basin. Water is carried home in small-necked clay jugs, balanced on the hip, and designed for a minimum of spilling. These public fountains are popular gathering places for gossip and social chatter and the women will stand talking together, idling and exchanging household views, long after the cool water has begun to turn warm in their jugs.

Water in Morocco is certainly a symbol of comfort and an assurance against the fears of thirst. One night, at about two o'clock, I was standing in a shabby section of Tangier, waiting for a taxi to take me back to the hotel. From behind the white walls of the narrow street came occasional sounds of life—a door slamming, a baby whimpering in its sleep, the faint murmur of a radio. Suddenly, from one of the doorways, appeared a woman, swathed and veiled as though it were midday. She carried a water jug. I watched her as she filled it at a fountain, then settled herself peacefully on the rim of the basin, trailing languid fingers in the water and humming to herself. Hers was a quiet, contented mood. Perhaps this was a nightly habit, a moment away from the family in the cool night air; pehaps she was an ultra-efficient housewife who wanted fresh water on hand for the morning mint tea. But it was evident what an important, soothing part this ancient, dripping fountain played in her life.

««««««««« »»»»»»»»»

There are movies and theaters in Morocco but only in the major cities such as Tangier, Rabat and other cosmopolitan areas. Morrocco makes no movies itself and hence has no national-hero movie stars of its own. Most Moroccan women and children simply do not go to movies (in fact, in Tangier there is *still* a law forbidding Moslem females to enter a cinema) because it is contrary to their sheltered customs. There is also a curious snobbery in some of the anti-movie attitude. A well-educated, emancipated teenager explained to me briskly, "That kind of thing is only for men and *servant girls*." She herself had only viewed one film, amateur pictures of a trip to Egypt, shown at a travel club.

And what kind of movies appeal to men and *"servant girls"?* For the later, favorites are stories shot in India and Egypt, with an easily-understood Arabic soundtrack, plotted (in the best soap opera tradition) about love, adventure and marriage among the poor and bedeviled. French movies, long popular among more sophisticated Moroccans, have recently been superseded by American films which now do double the volume of business of the French product. Cowboy movies have had an expected popularity but the most successful moving picture shown to date has been *The Vikings,* starring such non-Moroccan types as Tony Curtis, Kirk Douglas, and blonde, unveiled and lovely Janet Leigh. Not a sheik, pasha, or racing camel in the plot!

«««««««« »»»»»»»»

There is, in all Moroccan life, a strong feeling of sensuality and, because a man may legally take four wives, there are few females who are not married at some time or other. Perhaps it is partly this "enough for all" atmosphere that makes the women—veiled and unveiled—so interested in adornment and self-decoration.

Take a Berber girl in the countryside, for instance. As a little child, she is likely to be decked out in an ankle-length, belted sheath dress of pink, green or yellow satin. This garment invariably becomes tattered at the hem from trailing through brambles and hay stubbles, but the child, from infancy on, makes a bright, decorative spot on her landscape. As she nears adolescence, this country child may color her eyelids with blue gentian dust, rub her feet and the palms of her hands with red powdered henna (as does her mother) and draw dark, narrow lines over her eyebrows. At this age too, like her mother before her, she may have her forehead, chin and perhaps the tip of her nose tattoed in tiny, bright-blue patterns—dots, dashes or crisscrosses—according to the custom of her tribe. These tattoo marks, incidentally, are delicate and flattering—often pointing up the beauty of the eyes and skin or the whiteness of the teeth, just as do Spanish "beauty marks" or American eye make-up.

It is the mountain and desert women who wear the heaviest, most intricate jewelry and gaudiest colors. One day, a few miles out of Agadir, we turned our car into a dusty lane to check a map. Beside the road was a shallow pond, grown thick with rushes, and from behind these weeds sprang three teen-aged girls who had been bathing their feet in the water. The abrupt appearance, squeals of alarm and bright clothing made them seem like erratic, violently feathered water-fowl. It happened to be a feast day and these teen-agers were garbed in elaborate blouses and full skirts of red, blue and yellow, eyes ringed with blue powder, cheeks stained scarlet. Wrists and ankles jangled with chain and bead jewelry, and each girl was crowned with what can best be described as a "wig" of linked silver coins.

Again in the country areas, most of the jewelry is in coin shapes, hands of Fatima, or decorated chains. Earrings, either loops or chain-type, may hang down six inches from pierced ear lobes. Often beads and coins are strung on bright wool or stained leather cords to be worn as ankle and wrist bracelets. Occasionally, young bodies seem overburdened with the weight of "jewels," but the girls love the seductive, clanking music of their many decorations.

In the more sophisticated cities, where the women hide their finery under heavy robes and veiling, the jewelry is often less gaudy but of a better quality and more artistic design. And obviously a special excitement is engendered by the thought that a woman may be ornamented attractively but hidden from the eyes of the world, saving her glory for the privacy of her home. To a Moroccan woman, jewelry is not only a sign of wealth but an indication of her husband's affection, since usually it is received as a gift from him. I have been told that a wealthy Moroccan woman, when she does go visiting at another woman's home, will not only wear a vast collection of jewelry, but she will also carry the remainder of her treasures with her—to be spread out on the lap and admired during the visit.

«««««««« »»»»»»»»

"Casbah" means walled and can refer to an entire native quarter of any Moroccan city or to a single fortress type house of a wealthy landowner in the south. But in this country, almost every private dwelling is enclosured and even the most primitive Berber village is usually fenced in by a high hedge of prickly paddle-cactus.

The white, high-walled city houses, with a single, ironbound front door serving as entrance, are much like the Moroccan women themselves, covered over from the gaze of the world, with all ornamentation and treasure hidden inside. Home furnishings are fairly uniform, with house to house decorations differing in quality only. Quite naturally, a weathy man will select articles more expensive in workmanship and materials.

A typical Moroccan sitting room would probably be decorated with long wall hangings in dull pink, green or yellow satin, pointed and curved at the top of each panel in a "Moorish arch." These hangings, like the tapestries of medieval Europe, give color to the room and protect against the damp and cold exuding from the walls. Rugs, when used, are of heavy, hand-woven sheep's-wool, in the plain, natural color or zigzagged in designs of black and brown. These rugs are often woven with thickly tufted strips or with a high, soft nap that makes them excellent for sitting as well as walking on. Chairs are rarely used but big bolsters, placed against the walls, serve as couches, while hassocks or ottomans in the softest leather, dyed bright or etched with gold tracings, are set in convenient spots. Tables are infrequent and most meals are served off heavy brass trays set on tripods. The diners lounge on bolsters or squat on the floor. Niches in the walls serve to hold vases or other such ornaments but pictures are never displayed. White is the favored wall color and the rooms are usually tiled head-high in patterned squares; it is common to run a border of message-printed tiles along the top, with such petitions as "May Allah bless this family," or "May this house be free from scorpions." Moorish-type lanterns are known all over the world and the colored glass panels or intricately-cut iron frames cast colorful and patterned shadows over the already ornate room.

Moroccans are, on the whole, a very clean people and a room such as described here is easily tidied—tiles mopped fresh every morning, bolsters, pillows and hassocks plumped and whisked clean with a duster of feathers.

Bedrooms are extremely simple: large stuffed bolsters for

sleeping, a hassock or two and a big, trunk-type chest for clothing. Again, the wealthy home will show its opulence in wall hangings and embroidered spreads for the beds.

Some Moroccans have chosen to supplement their house furnishings with articles imported from France or England but the above native items are most common and most preferred. Cold, damp winter weather brings out the flat brass braziers, lit with charcoal or dried olive pits, to chase the chill from the rooms. In good weather, the total effect inside a well-run Arab home is one of fresh air, flowers, color, coolness and pleasant scents.

««««««««« »»»»»»»»»

The way of living and the furnishings in the mud-walled huts of a country village or *douar* are, of course, much more simple. Usually having not more than two rooms, such a home would likely contain a hand loom for weaving cloth and a hand mill for grinding corn, a mattress or rugs to sleep on and a few kitchen utensils such as water jars, a teapot —and a clay-saucer lamp with a wick for burning oil or mutton fat. Most cooking is done over an iron pot, fueled with charcoal or twigs and set just outside the door. At dusk, the cooking pots of a country village twinkle in the dark like fireflies.

The chief life of the farm family is lived outdoors, from early morning till sundown. At night, sheep, cattle and fowl are penned into rough enclosures close to the house. These are often made of closely planted cactus. By day, the animals graze in the open fields, tended by someone too young—or too old—for more arduous work. There are few fences in Morocco and this gives the land an open, endless look, as well as making custodians for the animals essential.

Men and women toil side by side in the fields, working most often with the same primitive-type tools employed for centuries—a forked, hand-guided plow drawn by a camel and donkey team, carved wooden pitchforks and hand-forged scythes. At threshing time, grains are brought to a treading area to be "threshed" by the hoofes of horses, mules, or camels. The wheat is then separated from the chaff by a laborious hand-sieving process. The broad, shallow sieves, incidentally, are often made of woven camel's hair.

If there is a running stream near the village, women do the family washing there, pounding the garments with stones or rubbing them with a grass-seed in place of soap. Young boys often help with the laundry chores, jumping up and down on the clothing with their bare feet, ultimately getting themselves as wet as the garments in the stream.

As a non-participant, one cannot be sure if Moroccan country life is as simple and peaceful as it looks, or if it is just boring. But against the background of beige fields and blue mountains, the figures of the farm families often make a restful and appealing picture.

«««««««« »»»»»»»»

Public baths are common in Morocco. Here, for a few cents, a man may rent a hook for hanging his clothing, plus a pail of soapy water, a towel and a scrub-brush. These baths are located just off the *souks* and they have big, darkened rooms to insure some privacy and slatted wood floors to slosh out the water. On Wednesdays, the baths are reserved for women only. The children and babies get tubbed out in the family courtyard, just as Americans took "Saturday night scrubs" in a galvanized tub with stove-heated water, in the not-too-long ago.

««««««««« »»»»»»»»»

We have talked several times about Moroccan clothing and how it differs from Arab to Berber, town to country. Here, by name and description, are some of the more common types of garments:

The *djellaba* is the ankle length, hooded robe worn by both men and women. It can be arranged over a complete dress or western-type suit. Men usually choose *djellabas* in solid white or grays; women prefer white wool or cotton or a gray-and-blue striping, like men's suiting for intown wear. The wearing of the *djellaba* is a fairly recent custom among Moroccan women and they are seen with it on only in larger towns.

The *haik* is the white, all-over, sheetlike garment worn by most adult females. It can be of any quality material but is most often made of coarse cotton and about twice the size of a regular double bedsheet. The voluminous *haik* is held on by a cord, which gathers in the material around several sides and then is pulled up and tied around the shoulders and under the arms, like a harness, leaving the wearer's hands and lower arms free. Some women prefer to go out in public without a face veil. They simply hold a portion of the fabric of the *haik* in their teeth, to cover the lower face.

The *'elettam* is the women's face veil, ranging in fabric from thick cotton to dainty lace. White is the favored color, though young women may choose blue or yellow, trimmed with a bit of embroidery. Unmarried women wear the *'elettam* just over the middle bridge of the nose; married women pull it up so it almost touches the lower lashes of the eyes. Very poor females sometimes "make do" with a simple rough bathtowel wound over the head and round the face, instead of veiling.

A *burnoose* is a heavy-fabric garment, often in wide black and brown stripes, worn by country men as a combination cover-all and blanket. It is loose-cut, with bat-wing arms and a hood, so a man can lie on the ground, cover himself from head to foot with a *burnoose* and sleep free from both sunrays and drifting sands. Since the *burnoose* is often woven from coarse wool still impregnated with natural sheep's oil, the fabric is almost completely waterproof.

The *fez, turban* and *tarbouche* are the common headgear for men. The first, familiar to us as part of the American Shriners' Convention regalia, is a stiff, deep red, felt pillbox, with a black tassel, usually worn with a western-type suit or *djellaba.* The *turban* is a graceful winding of cloth, in white or yellow, favored by older men. The *tarbouche* is a soft, brimless felt hat with a center indentation. This was the favored hat of the now-deceased King Mohammed V and is generally worn only by government officials or prosperous businessmen.

Babouches are the soft-leather, hard-soled and backless slippers worn by both men and women. They are excellent for sandy roads, rough cobblestones and hot weather, since they are both cool and easily slipped off for "emptying." *Babouches* are most frequently dyed yellow or such perky colors as poppy-pink and mint-green. The *slap-slap* sound of these slippers is as common to the casbah streets as the *tick-tack* of donkey hoofs.

Berber hats are giant straw cartwheels, meant to be decorative as well as keep off the sun. The heavy brims are held up by black wool cords attached to the center crown, and the straw is trimmed with red and yellow bobbles, colored cords and bits of mirror to glint and sparkle.

««««««««« »»»»»»»»»

Moroccans are generally highly superstitious people and the deeper into rural areas one goes, the deeper the superstitions. Some times these beliefs have religious bases, but more often they are just "inherited fears," handed down over long, long years, until superstitious folks believe them implicitly.

One "religious" superstition is demonstrated in the deep-country habit of shaving children's heads in intricate patterns. The most common practice is to shave the head almost totally, leaving a long tuft of hair on one side, to be braided into a pigtail. Even infants, with just a fuzz to work with, have their heads shaven in this lopsided fashion. The pigtail on children is believed to be a "handle to Heaven," a sturdy tuft to give Allah a good grip should he decide to yank the child up into Paradise. Some groups are accustomed to shave the child's head in "dots," making a series of little short-haired growths to please Allah. One *can* be carried away by the "oddness" of a new country. Once in Tangier, I noticed an infant strapped to its mother's back, the little head lolling and bobbling in a hat of crocheted gold threads. The tiny face was stained a deep purple. I mentioned to a doctor friend with whom I was walking that this seemed an extreme attempt to please Allah. He corrected me, after a close look at the child. "Not a superstition at all," he said. "This baby has impetigo and its mother has *wisely* painted the face with medicine!"

Life for the superstitious is also ruled by the "Evil Eye." All sorts of bad luck is blamed fearfully on the diabolic powers of "the Eye." A crop failure means that someone with the "Evil Eye" has gazed on one's fields; ill health befalling a house can be brought on by the "Evil Eye," and so forth. One day, in the poorer section of a casbah, I saw a group of pitifully ancient and crippled beggars reach for their crutches and totter away on painful limbs because a tourist had unwittingly pointed a camera at them, a truly "Evil Eye" which might bring further ill fortune.

Sometimes "Good Eyes" are used against "Evil Eyes," and many High Atlas tribesmen wear black coats with a huge red and yellow eye embroidered between the shoulder blades, to ward off evil from behind. "Good Eyes" are often woven in the patterns of rugs or fabrics. Wearing verses of the Koran around the neck, folded into a little leather amulet, is also believed an effective "Evil Eye" defense.

Fortunately for the peace of mind of the superstitious, the good luck symbol of the hand, more specifically the "Hand of Fatima," the daughter of the Prophet Mohammed, is considered an excellent protection against bad luck. A hand often appears in pictures painted over the doorways of houses, or in brass as a door knocker, or one is hung above the sleeping couch. Sometimes the hand is simply represented by five upright strokes, marked on a wall. If one suspects one is being stared at by an "Evil Eye," it is wise to raise a hand, palm outward, and say, "Here's five in your Eye." The five fingers of the hand are also believed to spell out the five letters in the name "Allah," thus drawing down his special protection. And, as we have mentioned, the "Hand of Fatima" is popular in jewelry. Almost every woman wears a "Hand" somewhere on her person at all times.

Certain other practices are believed to bring good luck: bread broken over the handle of the plow will insure fine crops, a ram's horn hung in a fruit tree will keep pests away from the harvest. There is a species of large flying locust, endowed with "good luck," which most Moroccans refuse to kill, even though it is injurious to vegetation. Mountain folk make little replicas of this insect in black iron with brass wings and keep them in their houses or tents to bring favorable luck.

Many Moroccans also believe in a hard-to-explain quality called *baraka,* which signifies "good fortune." Near every village, there are certain rocks, trees or caves which are thought to have *baraka* and which can sometimes pass it on to a believer who touches them. Most wealthy or important people, such as the king, have *baraka;* so do passive lunatics or simple-minded folk. (Once a lunatic becomes violent, however, he loses the mystical *baraka* and is locked up as dangerous.) Lions, white camels and racing greyhounds all have *baraka.* Saints or holy men possess *baraka* almost to excess and can pass on this quality to their shrines. Thus the countryside of Morocco is dotted with tiny, dome-roofed shrines dedicated to saints, where a prayer by a believer can hopefully produce *baraka.*

Baraka comes from Allah above and can be given or taken away at his wish. So when things are going well, *baraka* is present; when things go badly, *baraka* has been taken away. Thus—to a superstitious man—the blame for anything cannot fall on him. It is always the luck or fault of *baraka.*

«««««««« »»»»»»»»

Funeral customs vary greatly from faith to faith and the Moslem services are invariably simple but deeply religious affairs. The immediate care of the dead falls chiefly to family members but a holy man is usually called in to help, without fee. Burial is consistently performed within twenty-four hours after death, partly because embalming is not practiced in this country and partly because Mohammed has said that a righteous soul should not be kept apart from its awards in Paradise and a wicked man should be quickly put away.

Thus, immediately after death, a body is washed, scented and wrapped in fine cloth. During this process, verses from the Koran are chanted aloud by the holy man, family members and friends who have gathered at the house. Next the body, carried shoulder high on a simple wooden litter, is borne to the mosque, followed by mourners on foot, chanting verses from the Koran in unison. (Sometimes the body is carried in a simple pine box, but the litter is more usual). It is believed that angels precede the procession on foot, and thus it would be unseemly for the mourners to ride. I noticed that, after the recent death of King Mohammed V, his son, the new King, followed his father's bier on foot, according to age-old custom.

Moslems have a great respect for the dead and funerals and it is considered a privilege to help carry a coffin. Thus five or six relatives bearing the burden may be relieved on the way to the mosque by passers-by who wish to carry the body a few steps. This also insures a man who had died without family a dignified trip to the mosque.

Female relatives sometimes distinguish themselves from the rest of the crowd by carrying blue handkerchiefs which they whirl about their heads while marching. As pointed out before, frequently, women wail loudly and scratch their faces till blood runs, to indicate deep anguish. Wealthy Moroccans sometimes hire professional mourners to join the retinue, partly to suggest popularity of the deceased and partly, through their practiced lamentations, to aid the release of their true sorrow in inhibited relatives.

At the mosque, Koranic prayers for the dead are recited and then the funeral entourage proceeds to the graveyard, just outside the city walls. All bodies are intered without a coffin and after the shroud has been loosened; this is done in the belief that the sooner the body disintegrates to rejoin the earth from which it came, the sooner it will be joined with Allah.

In some homes, it is a custom to hire "readers" to visit the room in which the death occurred and there, for a period of about three days and nights, read the Koran aloud from beginning to end. Occasionally, very wealthy families distribute gifts to the poor in honor of the dead.

In short, the funeral customs—and costs—are simple ones and, though mourning may continue privately, it is presumed by all that the deceased is now experiencing joy and is truly "in the hands of Allah."

«««««««« »»»»»»»»

Moroccans are warmhearted family people, outgoing and affectionate, generally kind to children and regarding their numerous progeny as "blessed gifts from Allah." Because they consider marriage such an important and desirable goal, the customs in regard to betrothals and weddings have about them something of the joyous whoopla of a country carnival, rather than solemnity. Still, all preparations must follow the strictest traditions.

For instance, marriages are arranged directly between the parents of the potential couple, and negotiations and dowry discussions usually begin when a young man is seventeen or eighteen and his bride-to-be thirteen to sixteen. Quite naturally, both families will seek out mates whom they hope will be satisfactory for their children, both personally and financially. Thus most match-making takes place between families who are already friends.

To seal the engagement, the family of the groom will present gifts to the fiancee through her family, usually bolts of silk, perfumes, and, in the case of wealth, collections of jewelry. The bride, in turn, is expected to bring to the marriage all household linens as well as the collection of embroidered spreads, bolsters and cushions on which she has been sewing during her cloistered teen-aged life. For the first years of marriage, until a separate home can be afforded, most couples live with the parents of the groom.

It is possible that the young couple may have known each other in childhood, perhaps even have been playmates or lived on the same street for years. But once a girl has taken the face veil, no man outside her immediate family may look on her features. Thus a young man may not gaze at his fiancee's face until after the wedding ceremony. The teachings of the Prophet Mohammed have dictated the habits of Moroccan women for more than 1300 years, and most young girls are still guided by these words:

"And say to the believing women that they cast down their looks and guard their private parts, and display not their ornaments, except those which are outside; and let them pull their kerchiefs over their bosoms and not display their ornaments save to their husbands and fathers. . . .

"Oh ye women of the prophet! Stay still in your houses and show not yourselves. . . .

"Oh thou prophet! Tell thy wives and thy daughters, and the women of the believers, to let down over them their outer wrappers. . . .

"Men stand superior to women in that God hath preferred some of them over others. . . ."

«««««««« »»»»»»»»

In the cult of Islam, marriage is not a "religious sacrament" and is not officiated at by a "priest" or holy man. Rather, it is an earthly agreement between two people who make whatever vows and promises they wish privately and just between themselves. But this following quote from a famous Moroccan religious writer suggests what ideas are implicit in the marriage union:

"As regards propriety, one cannot be too careful not to let one's wife look at or be looked at by a stranger, for the beginning of all mischief is in the eye. As far as possible, she should not be allowed out of the house, nor to go on the roof, not to stand at the door. . . .

"If a man's wife be rebellious and disobedient, he should at first admonish her gently; if this is not sufficient he should sleep in a separate chamber for three nights. Should this also fail he may strike her, but not on the mouth, nor with such force as to wound her. . . .

"The Prophet said, 'If it were right to worship anyone except God, it would be right for wives to worship their husbands.' "

The Koran has laid down many edicts about the conduct of marriage and its associated problems. For instance, it clearly allows the taking of four wives at one time, but with the provision that each be treated equally in the household. Koran or no, economic pressures have reduced all but the wealthiest households to one or two wives, and educated Moroccan women have, in recent years, become more and more firm about being the only wife in a house.

The privilege of divorce is given solely to men and a man may divorce his wife simply by saying, "I divorce you!" three times. Under Koranic law, however, a man cannot remarry his divorced wife until she has *remarried* and been *divorced.* This proviso restrains a husband from divorcing a wife in a whimsical or facetious manner. On her wedding day, a young bride's family is paid one-third of a cash dowry promised by the groom's family; the remaining two-thirds must be paid *only* if the young man ultimately divorces his wife. Once again, economic pressure contributes to the stability of a union.

Again, under Koranic law, a man may put his wife to death or confine her to her chambers for life if he finds her guilty of unfaithfulness; but to prove the crime, he must provide four witnesses. Thus the Koran, in its ancient wisdom, adds a check to human emotions which might lead to tyranny.

«««««««« »»»»»»»»

Weddings are conducted as two-part ceremonies, with one celebration at the home of the groom, the other at the bride's. Let me describe, in brief, a wedding I attended in Tetuan, in northern Morocco. As a non-Moslem and friend of the groom, I was invited to his half of the ceremony and was the only female present.

Hassan was the seventeen-year-old son of a middle-class silk merchant, his bride the thirteen-year-old daughter of a tailor who lived just a few city blocks away. For the wedding, the courtyard of Hassan's house was a-blaze with extra lanterns and candles; freshly potted flowers lined the walls. The groom himself greeted us at the door, then guided us to a small sitting room off the courtyard, bending then to remove our shoes. Stocking-footed, we seated ourselves on a silken bolster, receiving grave welcoming nods from the dozen or more men already gathered about the room, also shoeless and puffing away on *hashish* pipes. In the courtyard, a group of musicians hunched on a straw rug, playing high, melancholy tunes on finger-drums, lutes and twangy guitars made from huge turtle shells. It was a warm summer night; the hour was eleven.

Generosity and good will were rampant throughout the celebration. After the usual ablutions, we were served mint tea and wedding breads, fine-grained baked rolls highly sweetened with honey. This preliminary feasting lasted a full hour. All services were performed by the groom and his three brothers and the quartet rolled brass trays, carried steaming teapots and presented baskets of bread in a fine sweat of hospitality. Later, we were served an enormous, elaborate and lengthy *cous-cous* feast, followed by melon and more mint tea. The celebration consisted of feasting, chatting and listening to the unexhaustible musicians; the mood was subdued but touched with strong suspense.

The night air was scented heavily with powders and colognes, flowers and the sweetish smoke of *hashish.*

In one corner of the courtyard stood an *almiryah,* a portable litter in which the bride was to be carried. It was painted green, cushioned inside with blue silk and hung with blue curtains. This *almiryah* had been rented, the groom explained; blue curtains had been selected because his mother hinted that blue was his bride's favorite color.

Meanwhile, at the bride's home, a gathering of female relatives and friends were feasting on *cous-cous* and helping to prepare the bride, adding touches of make-up and rearranging jewelry. Her wedding gown was blue, made from an engagement gift—a bolt of brocade. Moroccan wedding gowns are fashioned like floor-length coats, wide-skirted, long-sleeved and often held together up the front by gold frogs, like an ornate bathrobe. These wedding robes are extremely heavy, sewn over stiffening so that they could almost stand by themselves. For wealthy brides, the fabric is sewn over with gold threads and small patterns of jewels. Most sophisticated or city brides decorate themselves with heavy but not startling face make-up, powder, lipstick and eye darkeners that heighten the natural beauty without making the face grotesque.

At three in the morning, we guests at the groom's home began the joyous, noisy procession through the darkened streets of Tetuan to pick up the young bride. Four husky men carried the *almiryah,* balancing the four corners on their shouders. The musicians led the parade, playing as they walked, and the rest of the party, including the bridegroom, trailed along behind, carrying lit torches, many in the shape of the "Hand of Fatima," with a blazing candle protruding from each fingertip. Some of the more blasé guests simply swung lit flashlights as they walked.

As we neared the bride's home, a current of excitement spread through the group; the pace quickened until the musicians walked at a near trot and the *almiryah* swayed and rocked like a little rowboat.

At the bride's house, the groom and a female servant stepped inside. The rest of us milled around in the street; the band played loudly with all its stringy, flutey strength, certainly waking all the neighbors. A few moments later, the female servant stepped from the doorway, carrying the young bride, covered from head to toe and looking like an inanimate bundle of fine blue silk. The girl was placed in the *almiryah,* curtains drawn carefully, and all of us, rejoined by the bridegroom, trekked back through the streets.

Once more we caught sight of that little blue bundle as she was lifted from the litter and carried into the bridegroom's house. Then, after handshakes and final congratulations, we guests went our separate ways into the night.

Inside, the servant had carried her blue burden up to the bridegroom's chambers. There the young couple would look on each other's adult face for the first time and enjoy a special, private *cous-cous* feast. And thus would begin what was hoped, with the help of Allah, would be a long and happy life.

«««««««« »»»»»»»»

This wedding, in the Spanish-influenced town of Tetuan and arranged between two sophisticated, somewhat-educated families, was a dignified affair, though colorful, generous and abiding by tradition. It omitted the rather barbaric ceremonies often practiced in more primitive areas.

For instance, it is often the country custom for the groom to view his bride for the first time in the presence of her female relatives. The ceremony goes this way: the groom is led into a roomful of veiled and *yoo-yooing* females (that curious "*yoo-yoo*" is used as a sound for joy or sorrow), in the bride's home. Awaiting him is an ornate chair or a raised ottoman spread with embroidered robes to look like a throne.

After an appropriate pause, the bride's mother leads her daughter from an adjoining room. Following country practice, this girl's face is painted grotesquely, with skin made chalk-white, blobs of red on the cheeks and eyebrows marked with slashes of black. Her eyes are kept tightly closed, and she is required to turn around slowly three times in front of her bridegroom, arms stretched sideways. During this performance, the veiled mother makes a singsong sales talk, pointing out the thickness of her daughter's hair, the fairness of her skin and the grace of the body—although the young girl is almost shapeless in the cone-shaped wedding robe. The groom must watch this performance without comment or change of facial expression. After the girl's third revolution, he seizes her by the wrist—thus symbolically taking her as his wife—and leads her to a nearby room. The young couple's first hours together are spent just a few feet away from the noisy, curious women guests who stay on and on until the last possible bit of excitement has been gleaned from the occasion.

«««««««« »»»»»»»»

It is often said in Morocco that pious women leave the walls of their homes only twice—once at marriage, once at death. And both are noisy, conspicuous exits.

Chapter VI

ISLAM: "THERE IS NO GOD BUT ALLAH!"

MOROCCANS ARE—from dawn to dark and every day of the year a deeply religious people. Their religion is called Islam. Allah is their God, Mohammed is His Prophet and the Koran is the Holy Book. In adherence to their faith, Moroccans can range from devout to fanatic. Injunctions from Allah can touch nearly every phase of life, from method of prayer to treatment of dumb animals. In Morocco, Islamism is everywhere, all the time.

This religion may properly be called Islam or Moslem. It is sometimes referred to erroneously as Mohammedanism. Mohammed, called "the Seal of the Prophets" and considered the last of a long line beginning with Adam, the first man, is the major Prophet. But he is only the prophet and therefore this religion cannot properly bear his name.

Mohammed, according to tradition, was born in 570 A.D., in the town of Mecca, in what is now Saudi Arabia. He was called Mohammed ibn Abdulla ibn abd-al-Muttalib ib Hashim. As happens with many renowned men, especially those associated with religion and miracles, a number of legends arose about Mohammed's birth—but only after his death. Moslems now believe that on the night of Mohammed's entrance into the world, the heavens burst into glory, sending down a shower of stars, while the mountains of the area rocked and sang out the message, "There is no God but Allah!" and the valley lands responded, "And Mohammed is His Prophet!"

Because his father died before his birth, Mohammed was raised first by a grandfather and then by an uncle. As a boy he tended herds in the plains outside the city. His was a deeply pious home and there he heard a potpourri of stories about the religion of his people, based on centuries-old acquisitions and beliefs: Arabs were the direct descendents of Ishmael, Abraham's first-born son; Mecca (Mohammed's birthplace) was a sacred city because Adam, the first man, settled there after his exit from Paradise. On the spot where Adam first pitched his tent there stood the sacred shrine, the Kaaba. The Black Stone, called the Ruby of Heaven (the exact stone is still in existence), was set in the corner of this shrine after having been brought by Adam from Paradise and so on. Young Mohammed heard many stories and was told of many gods, represented by idols as was the custom of the times. The god mentioned most often was called Allah.

Though he was a deep thinker and had spiritual interests, Mohammed was not considered an unusual person in his youth. He worked as a caravan leader and was outstanding for his industry and devotion in that field, at least. At twenty-five, he married his employer, a widow fifteen years his senior. One daughter, Fatima, was born of this union. The wealthy wife, Khadijah, was pious, learned. Mohammed now had more time to meditate and study and began to spend long hours alone in the caves outside Mecca. It was there that, at the age of forty, the Prophet experienced his first vision.

In this visitation Allah, through the Angel Gabriel, ordered him to abolish idolatry in his country and organize a "One God" religion, with Allah as the Supreme Being. Legend says that Mohammed was terrified by the first vision, believing he was being taunted by the Devil. It was his wife, who urged him to pray for strength and guidance and to accept the role forced on him. Other visions followed, with further instructions and revelations, and Mohammed, inspired with zeal, recruited his first three disciples—his wife and his future son-in-law and father-in-law.

For more than a decade, Mohammed preached and proselytized in and around Mecca, urging people to give up idolatry, tribal feuds and semipagan rites and believe in the Will and Way of Allah. (The word "Islam," incidentally, means "submission to the will of God.) Gradually, men outside Mecca responded to Mohammed's message, but among unbelievers in the city, animosity grew until a plot was formed to kill the Prophet. In the summer of 622 A.D., Mohammed fled Mecca, only to return eight years later with a following of ten thousand, to destroy all idols and put the city under the religious rule of Islam.

When the Prophet died in 632 A.D., at the age of sixty-two, his followers began to gather together all his writings, the records of his visions, his revelations from Allah and his personal observations on life and religion. When the collection of revelations was completed, it contained 114 chapters, each representing one or more revelations. The latter were arranged according to length, from the longest to the shortest, regardless of the time sequence in which they were written. These writings comprised the Holy Book, the Koran, which in Arabic means "the Reading." From the Koran all the basic teachings and inspirations for present-day Islam are still derived.

Besides the Koran, the collected observations of Mohammed were brought together in a lengthy work called the Hadith or Table Talk of Mohammed. The Koran presents the final word on religion itself; the Hadith is used as a basic code for daily Moslem living. And Mohammed had a word to say on almost every subject.

Within a century, Islam had spread over Palestine, Egypt, North Africa and Spain and had even reached France. The venerated Moslem saint, Moulay Idriss, brought the teachings to Morocco and set up headquarters at his newly-established city of Moulay Idriss, near Fez, today the Mecca of Morocco.

«««««««« »»»»»»»»

The Moslem creed is "there is no god but God (Allah). Mohammed is His Apostle." Acceptance of this statement as a fact implies belief in 1) God, 2) the angels, 3) the inspired books, 4) the prophets, and 5) the day of judgment and God's predestination of good and evil. Anyone may become a Moslem simply by declaring his faith in these beliefs—and then following the other precepts of the religion.

Every true believer is obliged to perform the following practices: 1) recital of the creed, 2) performance of divine worship five times a day, 3) fasting in the month of Ramadan, 4) payment of alms and 5) the pilgrimage to Mecca.

The creed must be recited at least once in a lifetime, correctly and with full understanding and faith, as a "declaration of belief." The average Moslem would probably say the creed hundreds of times within his life span.

Prayer five times a day is required for every Moslem living a regular life; that is, in time of war or during an arduous journey, the prayer rules are not binding.

It is the practice of offering prayers five times a day that makes the permeation of Islam in Morocco so obvious to a traveler. One *hears* and *sees* the prayers everywhere. Prayer hours are dawn, just after noon, before sunset, just after sunset and just after the day has closed. The faithful are summoned to prayer by a *muezzin* who calls out his message over the city or countryside from the top of a high, slim minaret. At noontime, many men try to make their prayers in the local mosque but others pray wherever they happen to be, prostrating themselves with head pointed toward Mecca—in the farm fields, within workshops or along the roadside.

In the country, it is a moving sight at dusk to see figures bending and praying among the crops, workers who have stayed to toil till the last glint of sunshine has faded and then make their prayers to Allah just when He has taken away His light. There are many such instances that stay vividly in memory. For example, there was the time we looked out of the window of a high hillside palace in Tangier, and saw, far below, a minaret on whose platform a *muezzin* was only a tiny figure, singing out and holding up outstretched arms. A few moments after this last call to prayer, lights began to wink out all over the casbah. With a good-night message to Allah, part of the city was going to bed.

These prayers are ordinarily preceded by the *Wudu,* or minor ablutions, in which the believers wash their faces, their hands up to the elbows and their feet. As mentioned, each devotion is made in the direction of Mecca. In the mosques, Mecca is indicated by a special niche in the wall.

Entry to mosques is strictly forbidden to nonbelievers but one *can* peep through the open doors when passing. Also, I have visited the old Moorish mosque in Cordoba, Spain—now a Catholic church—and the huge, green-domed and active mosque in Kano, in Northern Nigeria. At Kano, a casual, nonbeliever guide just opens the door to anyone who wants to look inside—for a tip—but no stranger is allowed to be present during prayers.

Moroccans feel strongly about the sacredness of their mosques and few travelers would dream of violating their beliefs. But one day I did see a teen-aged American boy approaching the door of a mosque with a camera. An elderly Arab took him by the arm and spoke rapidly but kindly in Arabic. Not only was he attempting to enter a holy building, he was carrying a mechanical "Evil Eye." The boy obviously got the message—but refused to acknowledge it. He said loudly, "I am an American and we give money to you people. I can do anything I like!" In a matter of seconds, a group of Arab men had surrounded the boy and hustled him away from the mosque and a considerable distance down the street. There was no violence but the boy was definitely not allowed to enter the mosque.

I rather think religious belief was not the only principal at stake here. Someone probably understood the teen-ager's arrogant ill-advised English.

«««««««« »»»»»»»»

Most mosques are similar in interior design, a central vaulted roof, surrounded by a series of minor vaultings, all supported by rythmic rows of pillars. Inside the door, there is running water, with stone basins for ablutions. The floors are laid with straw mattings or prayer rugs, suited for kneeling and prostrate prayers. Besides the niche to indicate Mecca and some ornate hanging lanterns, there is often a small pulpit from which prayers can be led on special holy days. Some mosques have intricate plantings around the exterior, which may include well-tended fruit and flower gardens. The whole, inside and out, is designed to give a feeling of uncluttered calm, an inducement to meditation and true spiritual communion with God.

«««««««« »»»»»»»»

The instruction on fasting, as one of the "five pillars of faith" handed down by the Koran, begins with the words, "Oh ye who believe! There is prescribed for you the fast, as it was prescribed for those before you. . . ." The principal fast is observed during the month of Ramadan. This is the ninth month of the Moslem year and Mohammed is believed to have received the first of his revelations for the Koran from God on the Night of Power—the twenty-seventh day of Ramadan.

During this month, all the faithful, except children, the aged or ill, must abstain from food and drink from sunrise to sunset. The Koran states that, if one is on a journey during Ramadan, he may fast "another number of days" or if one *can* fast but prefers not to, he may receive partial blessing by feeding a poor man, but "if ye fast, it is better for you." Most Moroccan Moslems practice the month-long fast.

«««««««« »»»»»»»»

Centuries ago, the giving of alms was a complicated thing, depending on a man's crops and cattle and gathered in by official alms collectors. Today, however, the contribution of monies is left up to a man's conscience and help or money passed on to needy fellow-Moslem is interpreted as "alms." Most beggars feel confident of at least a few-cents' contribution if they cry out, "Alms! Alms in the name of Allah!"

«««««««« »»»»»»»»

The fifth religious duty of a devout Moslem is the pilgrimage to Mecca. This sacred journey should be made at least once in a lifetime, provided a man is physically capable and can provide for his family in his absence. There are three days in the year considered especially "blessed" for this practice and the rituals performed at Mecca are traditionally formalized.

When the pilgrim arrives within five miles of Mecca, he strips himself of his regular clothing and, after ablutions and prayers, dons two seamless wrappers. He then proceeds on his way without head covering or shoes. During the next three days, he must not shave, anoint the head, nor trim the nails. Next, the pilgrim must complete other rituals such as visiting the sacred mosque, kissing the Black Stone, encircling the *Kaaba* seven times—three times, running, four times slowly. There is also the hearing of a sermon and other pious observances. After all the ceremonies have been completed, the Moslem puts on his normal clothing and usually stays in Mecca another few days, sight-seeing and paying a reverent visit to the tomb of Mohammed.

In the times of the Great Prophet, Mecca—just forty-five miles from the Red Sea—was already an important city, serving as a commercial town for imported goods and as a congregating point for camel caravans. When Islam had its rise, much of the publicity for the new religion was carried out into the world through converted traders and caravaneers. These man took with them not only their new belief in one God but they spoke of these truths in Arabic. Hence Islam is now known among some of the most remote tribes in Africa, and their native speech has Arabic words scattered throughout.

Today, Mecca is a thriving city of about 100,000, surviving almost totally on its tourist pilgrim business. Centuries-old religious scholars' colleges, crowded around the sacred *Kaaba,* have long been turned into lodging places for wealthy tourists. And the city, through alms donations, maintains sleeping and dining quarters, and even a small hospital, for the poorer Moslems who manage to make the sacred pilgrimage.

This visit to Mecca, as we have mentioned, is an Islamic *duty* when a Moslem is physically able and can afford the trip. The custom draws the devout from every corner of the world. One afternoon, in the airport of Kano, Nigeria, one of the greatest airdromes of Africa, we followed a sign printed in English and Arabic reading: PASSENGERS FOR MECCA—THIS WAY. In a large, bright airport waiting room, furnished with chrome and plastic leather furniture, sat a group of between-planes pilgrims, ready for the next flight up to the Holy City. They ranged in skin coloring from bluest-black to very fair. Some wore Arab robes and turbans, others were dressed in gray flannel business suits and spent the waiting period going over papers from prosperous-looking briefcases. Tea was served—both mint and English—with little packets of biscuits wrapped in twentieth-century cellophane.

The drift of talk in the sunny waiting room was in more than a dozen languages; yet everyone in that lounge was caught up in the same excitement of a holy mission nearly accomplished. The words of Mohammed, the shepherd boy, have spread far over the earth.

«««««««« »»»»»»»»

Verses from the Koran and the Hadith are taught to Moroccan boys almost as soon as they can lisp out their first words. Girls are taught something of the Sacred Writings at home, but almost every boy, between six and nine, goes to Koran school. In fact, for many, this is the only schooling ever received.

The main purpose of these little schools, scattered everywhere throughout the cities' *medinas* and also in larger villages, is to help boys commit to memory as much of the Sacred Words as possible. In structure, the schools usually follow a similar pattern: one small windowless room, lit and aired by an open door, in which are crowded many little boys, sitting on the floor, reciting in singsong the verses called out by the teacher. Sometimes the children write out the words on a slate, spend some time in silent memorization, then recite in unison. Coming on one of these classrooms "in full voice" is like stumbling on a hive of noisy bees and the buzz and hum echoes up and down the crooked, narrow streets.

I remember one such school in Rabat. In spite of the brilliant sunlight outside, the inner room was so lightless that the boys' white teeth seemed to shine luminously as they recited. Their teacher, a lank, turbaned elder, sat slantwise near the open door, angling his big, bare feet out into the fresh air, wiggling his toes as if to catch a breeze. And the words of the Prophet echoed out through the whole length of that humid afternoon.

«««««««« »»»»»»»»

Just as the crosses a-top Christian churches reach toward heaven and spot the European landscape with their signs of faith, so the domes of mosques spot the horizons of all Morocco, the curved roofs more gentle in their "prayer attitudes." Mosques are usually the most dominant buildings in any city. Out in the country, a tiny place of worship often shows itself, tucked among a grove of trees, silent and remote, offering shade and a place for meditation to travelers and nearby country folk.

One of the most appealing mosques in all Morocco is set on

a low mountaintop at a place called Sidi Sin, about sixteen miles outside of Tangier. Sidi Sin is an excellent example of how religion works its way in-and-out of Moroccan life, because this location is not only a holy place but a favorite family social spot as well.

On Friday mornings, rickety buses bring whole families here for a two-day "religious picnic." The mountain is a series of gentle peaks, topped by a heavy growth of firs. It looks out over rolling grain fields to distant hills, offering a vast view that has about it the symmetry of peace.

On the top of the highest peak, and completely hidden from view by pines, sits the Sidi Sin mosque. As a female and nonbeliever, I was not allowed to approach within seeing distance of the sacred edifice but have been told that it is of white stone, green roofed and surrounded on three sides by tiny, cell-like rooms for unmarried men.

On the lower slopes of the mountain, families arranged tents by simply winding bed sheets around trees to make four-sided, unroofed shelters. Rugs were spread on the ground and veiled women chatted and watched over little children while the men folk strolled or sat in the shade, playing checkers on a "board" sketched in the dust, using soft drink bottle caps for "checkers." On the flat plain at the foot of the slopes, older children amused themselves at tag, soccer or tenpins, rolling a big rubber ball against a row of soft-drink bottles.

Each family brought its own food for the sojourn and no peddlers or commercialism were allowed. Live chickens or ducks were tethered in the shade, and heaps of melons cooled in hollows in the earth. After nighttime prayers in the mosque (for men only), it is the custom for all the unmarried men to roost themselves in trees on the upper mountain while the married women and the maidens stand on the plain. Then the group sings, sometimes in unison, sometimes with one or the other group echoing out refrains or choruses.

On one side of the mountain there is a source of good, fresh water, considered blessed. This water is the reason for the lush fertility of the mountain, and it also supplies the pilgrims for their weekends. It flows from the ground as a quiet, steady stream which ends in a deep, natural well, cupped on three sides by artificial stone basins to give easier access. In the late afternoon sun on the day of my visit, the pool looked more sluggish and tepid than sacred. But it must have been remarkably health-giving; the water was shot through with a formidable growth of outsized tadpoles!

«««««««« »»»»»»»»

The most important "feast" on the Islamic calendar is Ramadan, the month-long combination of feast and fast. The fast is proscribed in the Koran, as we mentioned, and lasts—for every adult, able-bodied Moroccan—from sunrise until sunset. The Holy Book poetically states it this way: "Eat and drink until so much of the dawn appears that a white thread may be distinguished from a black, then keep the fast completely until night."

No food of any kind may be taken during this period and no liquids, not even water. Cigarettes and hashish are also forbidden. In a hot country, the no-liquid rule can produce very genuine deprivation, even if only observed in a twelve-hour fast. Many Moroccans try to reverse their living patterns during Ramadan, sleeping through the daylight fasting hours and eating and working at night. For many merchants and businessmen, this arrangement is not possible, however, and at the Ramadan season tempers are often noticeably short. During the years when their control in the country was slipping, the French, were particularly alerted at the time of the fast, since riots and aggressions against them were always more frequent during this period.

Even Mohammed, centuries ago, had a word of warning to give on the subject of "tensions during Ramadan": "Keep fast and eat also, stay awake at night and sleep also, because verily there is a duty on you to your body, not to labor overmuch, so that ye may not get ill and destroy yourselves; and verily there is a duty on you to your eyes, ye must sometimes sleep and give them rest; and verily there is a duty on you to your wife, and to your visitors and guests that come to see you, ye must talk to them.

"Illumine your hearts by hunger, and strive to conquer yourself by hunger and by thirst; knock at the gates of Paradise by hunger."

«««««««« »»»»»»»»

Rather than use the "thread test" to determine the end of the day's fast, most Moroccans depend on the action at the minaret to tell them when the sun is truly down. A white flag flutters on top of each tower, to be taken down when the sun sets. At that moment, too, the *muezzin* gives out his usual sunset call to prayer.

Watching for the flag to fall, Moroccans often stand in home doorways or along *socco* streets like foot racers waiting for the starting gun. The favorite food for breaking the fast is, as we mentioned in the chapter on food, the hot, thick *herrira* soup. Vendors with buckets of this thick broth stand waiting for the exact moment to start selling. Some men, with more controlled appetities, break the daily fast first with a glass of cold water and a contended cigarette, then go home to feast in earnest.

Every house that can afford it serves Ramadan feasts of roast mutton and special *cous-cous*. A large portion of the dark hours is spent (by the men) visiting from home to home, roaming the streets or playing cards in cafes. Frequently, little bands, with drums and flutes, parade through the casbah, and the noise and celebrating lasts all night, every night of the month.

These celebrations never include alcoholic beverages. Mohammed has said "no," and I was interested to find, in the Hadith, what a decisive, outspoken prohibitionist he was: "The Prophet hath cursed ten persons on account of wine: first, the extractor of the juice of the grape for others; the second for himself; the third the drinker of it; the fourth the bearer of it; the fifth the person to whom it is brought; the sixth the waiter; the seventh the seller of it; the eighth the eater of its price; the ninth the buyer of it; the tenth that person who hath purchased it for another."

In short, no liquor. Period.

«««««««« »»»»»»»»

The second great feast of Islam is called Bairam, or The Feast of the Sheep, and it falls during the summer. Bairam is considered a time of peace, a holy day on which all feuds must be forgotten, all quarrels patched. For several days before the holiday, the market place is crowded with live sheep, for every family tries to have its own animal to roast. Of them the residential streets resound with the plaintive bleating of sheep tethered in courtyards or inside gardens, fattening up for the spit.

Wealthy Moroccans like to buy new clothing to garb themselves afresh, from head to foot, for Bairam. Others will make certain that their best garments are washed and attractive.

Everyone likes to wear at least a new, brightly-colored pair of slippers, just as many of us insist on a flowered hat or chic suit for the Easter Parade.

On the day of The Feast of the Sheep, a sacred procession winds its way out from the center of each town, headed by a horseman bearing a banner in green, the sacred color, and followed by the King's representative guards, and an entourage of city officials, all colorfully uniformed and excellently mounted. After them, on foot, may follow "holy men" and other males of the locality, carefully groomed for the day. The procession wends its way to a plain outside of the town, designated as the prayer-field, at which spot the women and children have already gathered. Prayer services are conducted, lasting about an hour, and then comes the great moment of the day.

A sacrifical sheep is led forth and a sharp knife is plunged into its throat. Then a single gunshot is fired, to indicate to all within hearing that the knife has been thrust. The dying sheep is instantly loaded into a huge straw basket and rushed on horseback to an appointed mosque in town. It is believed that, if the sheep is still alive on arrival, this augurs well for a happy, peaceful year for all Morocco and a second gunshot is fired outside the mosque to signal the good news. If the sheep should be dead on arrival, crops will fail and evil probably befall the land. At the moment of the second gun firing, or just after the bleeding sheep has been spirited away, each Moroccan at the prayer-field will take his neighbor's hand and touch his own lips with his own fingers in the salutation of peace.

Today, with cities spreading to unprecedented size, streets filled with heavy traffic, etc., the sheep may or may not reach the mosque alive, and the second gunshot may be dispensed with altogether. After all, who could hear it above the other noises of the twentieth century? But Allah is good—and it is customarily presumed that the sacrifice has been "accepted," and the year will be a prosperous one.

The rest of the day is spent in butchering and cooking individual sheep at home, sipping mint tea and offering the hospitality of one's home to friends and neighbors.

«««««««««« »»»»»»»»»»

I have never been in Morocco on the day of The Feast of the Sheep but was lucky enough to spend the holiday once in Fort Lamy, a small town in French Equatorial Africa. There are many Moslems there and it was interesting to see that they followed the prescribed rituals and prayers for the feast exactly.

For several days before the event, the primitive open-air market places were tethered solid with a kind of sheep peculiar to the locale—animals divided into two colors by a line running around the midriff and marking them almost exactly in two, half chocolate and half vanilla. At dawn on the feast day, the bush paths around the whole countryside streamed with the faithful on their way to the prayer-field. The men, who might wear nothing but a loin cloth on most days, were dressed in Moslem fashion, spotless white robes and twisted turbans. Many were accompanied by womenfolk, Moslem in faith perhaps, though not only unveiled but totally naked from the waist up. There was a mixed, but not inimical, atmosphere in town—a combination of holiday fever and supreme peace.

After the performance of the Islamic rites, these Equatorial Africans added some attractions of their own. There were troops of enuch dancing boys, artifically blinded and clothed in skirts and face-veils of finely strung colored beads, also wandering musicians playing eerie tunes on homemade xylophones, constructed from thin boards and underhung with gourds filled in varying densities with spiderwebs, to give changing tones. At the peak of noon, in the square beside the mosque, hundreds of Moslems lifted their long skirts to do a wild, prolonged spear dance derived from their more primitive jungle days. Spears, however, were replaced by cane poles, since the French frown on "group weapons," even on a traditionally sacred day of peace.

In this small desert town, one was able to watch the wounded sheep, very much alive during the journey, lugged to the mosque by some husky runners. Its slow demise promised a good year for the community. A second slash to the throat ended its suffering and a holy man used the same knife to hack the animal to pieces, distributing the meat to the poor.

In town, (as the home-slaughterings began) the open-faced gutters bordering each street ran with sheep's blood. And the blood that didn't run soon began to coagulate and rot in the hot African sun. It was a feast day for the vultures, too, and the streets were marked with the swooping shadows of great, black wings.

The festivity and merrymaking filled the streets of the town and the plains around it, but all the *feasting* seemed to take place inside huts or behind white walls. I was immensely curious to taste the roast sheep (our tiny French hotel was serving baked trout, green salad and an assortment of cheeses) but was unable to break through the hospitality barrier. *Bairam* may be a feast of peace and love for Moslems —but there was not one Son of the Prophet who would offer a bit of roast mutton to this unbeliever.

««««««««« »»»»»»»»»

"Moslems are brothers in religion and they must not oppress one another, nor abandon assisting each other, nor hold one another in contempt. The seat of righteousness is the heart; therefore that heart that is righteous, does not hold a Moslem in contempt; and all the things of one Moslem are unlawful to another, his blood, property and reputation."

These are the words of Mohammed as recorded in the Hadith or Table Talk of Mohammed. The sentiments expressed advocate charity and consideration for others; but even in this short injunction, the word "Moslem" is stressed three times. In Morocco, while a Moroccan may be righteous toward Moroccan Moslems, he does not often hold the same just attitude toward his fellow Moroccans, but traditional enemies, those of the Jewish faith.

For centuries, the Jew in Morocco has been treated with contempt and he is often subjected to special and harsh laws. Under the French protectorate, the Moroccan Jew could live in comparative dignity and business security. But today, as in centuries past, the Moroccan Jew is often the subject of derision and out-and-out discrimination.

We have mentioned that the Jews live in special sections of every town, called *mellahs,* a name derived from the salt tubs in which old-time Jews were compelled to salt the heads (cut off, of course) of political or personal enemies of powerful Moroccans. Today, many of these *mellahs* are the most wretched, crowded and poverty-ridden sections of any city. It is true that in the United States, in many of our larger urban areas, we too have slums where economically underprivileged people and certain racial minorities are wont to crowd together; *but* we are *troubled* by these conditions. These people are not required by law in our nation to live in proscribed areas and we are constantly building housing developments, issuing relief monies and generally studying the problem in an attempt to solve it. But in Morocco, except among a very few enlightened people, dislike and oppression of the Jew is considered a natural and guiltless thing. After all, a Jew is a nonbeliever.

Here are some of the statutes governing Moroccan Jews which were enforced fifty years ago:

1. They are never allowed to wear the turban. 2. They must wear black shoes instead of yellow ones ordinarily worn by Moroccans. 3. When they go from their own section of town into the Moorish section, Jews must remove their shoes and walk barefoot. 4. A Jew, meeting an Arab, must always pass to the left. 5. Jews are not allowed to ride within the city. 6. They are not permitted to carry arms. 7. They are forbidden the use of the Moorish baths. 8. In the practice of their religion, they are restricted to private houses; thus no public building may be used as a synagogue.

Today, the Jews certainly are allowed their own synagogues and, in many cases, their own schools. Under the French, many Moroccan Jews sent their children to French-run schools and thus have created an especially literate upperclass of Jews. But Morocco's 200,000 Jews today are constantly troubled by a trapped feeling and the fear of not knowing how or when new oppressions may be exercised against them.

For instance, it is almost impossible for a Jew to receive a passport to leave the country at all. In the early days of the founding of the new nation, Israeli, Moroccans who could scrape sufficient funds together *were* allowed to migrate and about 120,000 did. Now, all migration to the Promised Land is forbidden. Today, in fact, no communication is allowed between Morocco and Israeli. The Moroccan post office will refuse to accept any mail addressed to Israeli and will confiscate any mail coming in from that country. This has created a peculiar hardship, since many of the early emigrees are now completely out of touch with families still living in Morocco, and vice versa. And almost every Moroccan Jewish family has some relatives in Israeli.

In the fall of 1960, a decrepit yacht capsized in the Mediterranean. The story of that ship reached newspapers round the world. The boat carried some fifteen Moroccan Jews who had smuggled themselves out of their native country and were sailing toward the freedom of Israeli. All were drowned. Rumor spread through Morocco that a fleet of Jewish-manned vessels had sunk, not fleeing the country, *but sailing toward it for an invasion!*

In various parts of the nation, small riots broke out. Jewish shop windows were broken and Jews were beaten in the streets. In a few days, tensions eased—but no official word came from the government, offering clarification of the true situation or easing the concern of the Jews.

Often the discrimination is of a trivial but distinctly irritating, unjust sort. On one occasion, I inadvertently took part in a bit of this. In a *souk* one day, I was walking with a young Arab friend. He nudged me to stop and watch a lantern-maker at work. The man, head covered with a tiny black skullcap, was seated on the ground, cutting a design into a big tin Wesson oilcan, making an intricate fretwork of openings for light. Beside him stood several finished products, painted black and wonderfully artistic. We watched for several minutes before I said to my Moslem friend, "Beautiful work!"

He answered with irritation, "Not *work*. Look at him. Him funny. Him Jew!" So to this Moslem, typifying the attitude of many, this Jew—even though a talented craftsman, minding his own business—was just funny, an object of derision. A Jew!

In fairness, it must be pointed out that similar tensions and attitudes of *Jews* toward *Arabs* exist in some other North African countries. It is an age-old problem of religious rivalry for which a solution is being fervently sought; enlightened Arabs and Jews alike would prefer more harmonious relationships.

«««««««« »»»»»»»»

The sayings attributed to Mohammed, and recorded in the Hadith, range from verses wise and poetically stunning—to others that are just statements of "common sense." So all-encompassing are these verses that a devout Moslem can look to them to find the Prophet's opinion on almost any personal problem. Here is just a scattered sampling of Mohammed's advices.

"The proof of a Muslim's sincerity is that he pays no attention to matters which are not his business."

"To honor an old man is to show respect for God."

"Verily there is a heavenly reward for every act of kindness to a living animal."

"God is pure and He loves purity and cleanliness."

"Charity is the duty of every Muslim. If he has nothing to give, let him do a good deed or abstain from doing and evil one."

"Riches do not come from an abundance of goods but from a contented mind."

"When three persons are together, two of them must not whisper to each other without letting the third hear, because it would hurt him."

"God loves those who are content.

"He is the most perfect Muslim whose disposition is best liked by his own family."

"Do not drink wine, for it is the root of all evil; abstain from vice; and cherish your children."

"Every child is born with a natural inclination toward Islam. It is his parents who make a Jew, a Christian or a Magian out of him."

"God is gracious to him who earns his living by his own labor."

"Give the laborer his wages before his perspiration is dry."

"All should marry who can."

"Who is learned? They who practice what they know."

"He who repents sincerely is as one who committed no sin."

"The taker of usury, and the giver of it, and writer of the papers and witness to it, are equal in crime."

"He will not enter Paradise who behaves ill toward his servants."

"A virtuous wife is a man's greatest treasure."

"Deliberation in undertaking is pleasing to God, and haste is pleasing to the devil."

"My religion is like clouds dropping much rain; some of the drops, falling on pure, favorable soil, cause fresh grass to grow; some of them fall in hollows from which mankind are benefited; some fall on high lands from which benefit is not derived; then the two first are like the persons acquainted with the religion of God and instructing others; and the last like the person not regarding it nor accepting the right path."

«««««««« »»»»»»»»

It is more than 1300 years since Mohammed left the Meccan cave after his first vision and whispered to his wife the ideas of a new one-god religion. The Prophet believed that Allah had bade him preach Islam and that religion has been spread until today it is burgeoning with a new, vital growth.

Islam was born in Arabia, penetrated to France, Spain, India and a dozen other countries and permeated totally what is today the Arab world. For centuries, the whole of North Africa, from Morocco to the Red Sea, has been held together by the common bond of religion.

Now Islam is sweeping through the recently liberated countries of sub-Sahara Africa. Much of the new Africa is run and ruled by Moslems. *Moslems are successful.* Out of the entire population of Africa (232 million people) it is estimated that 90 million are Moslem, 77 million pagans and some 41 million are Christians. And today, for every African pagan turning to a new religion, one becomes a Christian, ten become Moslems.

Islam can be joined by a simple profession of faith and the following of specified practices without a long instruction period beforehand. It does not outlaw polygamy, which is so much a part of African life. With the withdrawal of the Christian colonizers such as France, Belgium and England, Islam has emerged as the "black man's religion," giving a oneness of belief to much of the continent.

Morocco, of course, has been Moslem for centuries but, suddenly, new brothers in religion, from Cape Town to Kenya, are chanting the same verses, honoring the same God, bowing to the same Holy City and making Africa ring out anew with the creed: "There is no God but Allah. Mohammed is His Prophet."

Chapter VII

"ARRIBA ESPAÑA!"— "DOWN WITH THE MOORS!"

Morocco—like most great nations—can look back in history on its "finest hour." And Morocco's finest hour, in terms of influence and conquest, stretched over a seven-hundred-year period, when that country penetrated into Spain, almost up to France, to impose Moorish customs, laws, civilization and even their Islamic religion on the Iberian peninsula.

The invasion through the straits of Gibralter started in the 700's. It began with a combination of violent emotions, intrigue and treachery. The story is that Count Julian, the Spanish governor of Ceuta, today a city in northern Morocco, had sent his beautiful young daughter to Toledo, to be educated at the royal court. The resident ruler at Toledo, one King Roderick, was long on passion and short on protocol. Some time later, the young girl smuggled a message down to her father in Morocco that she had been sullied by the King in a manner most unbecoming to a Spanish gentleman. In revenge, Count Julian allowed a Moorish scouting party to land in Spain through Gibraltar, reconnoitre—and, one year later, to invade successfully.

The military invasion took seven years; the more total cultural invasion took a full seven hundred. The Moors came to fight and stayed to raise families, till the soil, build mosques and bask in the fragrant, orange-scented sunshine of a country they have never ceased to love—and long for.

Only in the last decade have devout Moslems dropped from their regular evening prayers a plea to Allah to "restore to us Granada," that lovely mountain garden spot in southern Spain!

«««««««« »»»»»»»»

In many ways, the Moorish people never totally left Spain. Especially in the south, the dark hair and eyes, the passionate protection of women and the fiery pride of men seem a heritage of the Moors. To me, the close chaperonage of unmarried girls in Spain seems nearer to present-day Moroccan customs for women than it does the influence of Catholicism, the national religion of Spain.

In a few remote hill towns in Spain, even today, women are veiled in the streets in Moroccan fashion, and there is one primitive area above the southern coast town of Almeria where the women do all the farm work and herding of goats while the men stay at home as honored "males," as was the custom there during the Moorish invasion.

«««««««« »»»»»»»»

Water, as we have mentioned, has always been important to arid-country Arabs, and it is also very important in many dry areas in Spain. In the rural south, farmers still use the "Arab method" of irrigation in small fields, hoeing neatly parallel lines of earth between plants, with earthen barriers at each end. These barriers or "water gates" are laboriously opened and shut with a hoe to allow water to flow on, as one after the other of the furrows fills with water.

In bustling, modern Valencia, an old Arab-founded "water court" still holds sessions, just as it did one thousand years ago. Once the land around Valencia was arid and barren. The Arabs first instituted irrigation and water control here and today it is one of Spain's richest orange and rice growing areas.

At twelve noon every Thursday, in an ancient section of the city, the "water court" is called to order by the chiming of a clock in an old Moorish tower. The court is presided over by eight judges, or water authorities, one man for each of the eight main irrigation ditches through which Valencia's farm water is channeled.

These judges get no pay but are selected periodically from the wisest, most advanced farmers of the area. Only the good will toward the court gives their decisions weight—but no decision has ever been turned down. This independent court has no legal jurisdiction, yet its "decrees" have been carried out faithfully by landowners and rice planters of Valencia since it was first set up.

At the twelve stroke, the judges, in long, black robes, proceed in single file to the cathedral gates, there to be seated in eight ancient wooden chairs. The back of each is carved with the insignia of the ditch it represents.

There are no lawyers here and each farmer, plaintiff and defendant, presents his own case. Most frequently, the complaint is that Farmer A has used the water too long to let Farmer B get his fair share. (Irrigation ditches have shut-off gates at each farm.) When the total case has been discussed in terms of current rainfall, size and type of crop, season of the year, etc., a judge makes his decision. When all cases have been heard, the water court is adjourned until the next week.

So Valencia's irrigation waters have flowed, so crops and farmers' rights have been protected since a group of water-wise Arabs set up this court in 900 A.D.

«««««««« »»»»»»»»

The Moors left their architectural mark over the face of Spain, though more especially in the south. In Seville or Cordoba, for instance, one walks through tiny, crooked streets, passing high, blank white walls of houses exactly like those in a casbah. Through a grilled gate one may sometimes glimpse an "Arab" garden, with tiled floors, potted plants and tinkly fountains. Even the climate here seems to have been left behind by the Arabs, with summer days as hot and humid as nearer the Sahara.

The Moroccans believe the color "blue" is a deterent against intense heat and many hillside villages in Morocco use a tinted-whitewash, colored a bright, dusty blue for both inside and outside the houses. (I remember, incidentally, a forlorn little graveyard in Tangier in which the tombstones were also painted blue. Against the heat of the next world, perhaps?) In rural mountain-Spain, where some entire villages are housed in caves hewn from rock, the exact shade of Moroccan blue colors the doorways and interiors.

«««««««« »»»»»»»»

It is in its grand architecture, however, that Morocco—though unwillingly—gave its greatest gifts to Spain. The relics of the Moorish days on this peninsula are still among the finest treasures in the land.

In Cordoba stands the famous mosque, now consecrated as a Catholic Church, but so Moorish and distinctive in its architecture that Allah might well still be honored within.

The mosque sits in a spreading garden of orange trees, trimmed into plump green balls and with a fragrance as strong an incense. The mosque itself, built in the eighth century, is more beautiful than any mosque standing in present-day Morocco. Here the artistry and craftsmanship of centuries of mosque builders seem to have reached their peak.

Inside, the vaulted roofs are maintained by a breath-taking forest of 850 red and white jasper columns. The whole is so constructed that one sees in every direction a perfection of symmetry and precision. Several highly ornate Christian altars now stand here, but the prevailing mood is still one of Moslem "peace through perfection." Centuries ago, Moslems must have bent in prayer in this edifice, to thank Allah not only for health and prosperity in Spain—but also for this flawless building in which to deliver their prayers.

In Seville, that city of grilled windows and year-round geraniums, the Arabs left another architectural monument, the Giralda (the Weathercock). The old mosque there was razed and the present cathedral built in its place but the Moorish minaret, the Giralda, still stands. It is now topped by a bell-tower and a mammoth statue of Faith but the major building contribution is still Arabic.

In other old buildings in the city, Ancient Arab inscriptions in tile have been interspersed with random Christian motifs —so superficial have been some of the changes in decorations.

«««««««««« »»»»»»»»»»

We do not ordinarily think of today's Moroccans as gifted engineers, yet in the Spanish mountain town of Ronda there still stands a curved stone bridge which they built more than a century ago. It is rightly called "the old bridge" and spans the abrupt river chasm of the Guadiaro, about 530 feet deep and 330 feet wide. This structure shows the labors of three types of workmen over the centuries; first the Roman, then the major work of the Moors, and then repairs by Spaniards.

Near this river, too, are the well-preserved ruins of a Moorish palace, colorfully tiled, gracefully arched and with slim balconies overlooking the river. When the Arabs ruled Spain, they autocratically divided it into areas of control, fought over and ruled by force among themselves. Each triumphant leader set himself up a kingdom, then built and lived like a king. Hence a small town such as Ronda has its own centuries-old palace.

«««««««« »»»»»»»»

In all Morocco itself, there does not stand a more beautiful relic or a better example of Moorish architecture and workmanship than the famous Alhambra Palace in the Spanish city of Granada. Here there is everything that is distinctively Moroccan—the delicate pillars, the horseshoe arches, lush gardens, superb fountains and colorful tile work.

This famous palace-fortress was built in the thirteenth century by the Moors and took more than a hundred years to complete. Some say the name "Alhambra" comes from an Arabic word meaning "red"—and much of the building is in a fine, reddish brick. Others say the "red" refers to the glow of torchlights under which night-work was done for years, sending a red light out over the valley.

Today, only part of the Alhambra still stands but that is in excellent repair. Much of the great building was torn down and carted off over the years, to be used in constructing Christian churches.

From the hills on which it is located, the Alhambra looks out over Granada, the deep valley-gorge cut by the river Daro and the surrounding countryside. The peak-arched windows of the building were deliberately constructed as delicate "frames" for the scenes beyond. Some window scenes are filled with carefully planned garden plantings of jasmine, myrtle and orange trees, interspersed with fountains. Other windows show the great natural beauties of distant plain and mountains.

One of the most famous rooms of the Alhambra is the Hall of the Abencerrages, a perfectly square room with a lofty dome, all decorated in blue, red, gold and brown and edged by delicately trellised windows. It was customary, and still is, for Moroccans to decorate and carve their ceilings with great artistry. Since much leisure time is spent reclining on bolsters, one of the best views is always "up."

Legend has it that the refined beauty of this particular room was once marred by a short-tempered Moorish king of Granada who had prepared a feast for one hundred of his chiefs in the Hall—waited till all were served and then ordered their massacre.

The Court of the Lions, just off this room, is more famous and more architecturally inspiring. It is an elongated oblong area, surrounded by a low gallery supported by 124 white marble columns. The courtyard and part of the walls are covered with yellow and blue tiles and the whole is centered by a white alabaster pool, guarded by twelve white marble lions, symbolic of courage and strength. This courtyard combines several features which Moroccans, to this day, value as beautiful—fresh air, open sky and constant running water.

The lower chambers of the Alhambra show fascinating remnants of old harem life at its most lavish. Here stand excellent remains of deep stone bathtubs, with ingenious wall openings to spray out scents after the cleansing. Adjoining the baths are the once-elegant chambers where Moorish men might entertain their favorites. Visitors will find stone wall-benches, once covered with cushions and damask, while around one wall runs a narrow balcony from which played sightless musicians, deliberately blinded so they might not look on the loveliness of the ladies below!

«««««««««« »»»»»»»»»»

The Spanish, who went on to conquer a few worlds of their own after freeing themselves from Moorish yolk, still bear traces of their conquerors in the tone of their speech—and in some of the things they say. The voices of many unschooled southern Spanish ring with the nasal, singsong intonations of the Arabs; and in the south, some of the fiercest curses and swear-words are in Arabic. Even some of the brief prayers for "luck with the catch," called out by Spanish fishermen, are in Arabic, though addressed to a Christian God, rather than to Allah.

In Spain, I have often been amused to be told a centuries-old "rumor"—that Moroccans still hold keys to many of the ancient buildings in such places as Cordoba and Seville and are just waiting for the day they can return to take over. Occasionally, too, Spaniards will explain the hardships or barren soil of a mountain village as being due to "a curse put on the place by a Moor."

«««««««««« »»»»»»»»»»

Little by little, the Moroccans, over a period of half a century, were driven back toward the Mediterranean, until they lost their domination in Spain completely in 1492. Capitulation came because the Arabs lacked central organization and their leaders had grown soft on luxury. But it was not until the Catholic rulers, Ferdinand and Isabella, were in full power that the last Arab was "driven into the sea."

Of course, all the Moors did not leave on defeat. Moorish power was broken, but over the seven-hundred-year span of dominance, many had intermarried with Spaniards and had no wish to leave. Those who stayed were required to become Christians and, as time has gone on and on, became as Spanish as the Sierra Nevada Mountains.

There is an old saying, "Africa begins with Spain," and that seems quite natural, since so much of Africa is still there.

«««««««« »»»»»»»»

The discovery of America is also closely linked with the defeat of the Moroccans in Spain. Had the Moors fought even harder and longer, Queen Isabella—so involved in the planning of the bitter fighting—would not have had time to listen to the pleadings of Christopher Columbus for money and ships. In fact, the Queen kept the greater explorer waiting six years before she finally agreed to finance his venture to the new world. It was in the Moorish Alhambra, kneeling on Moroccan tiles, that Columbus made his final and successful plea to Isabella.

«««««««« »»»»»»»»

Even today, modern Moroccans speak lovingly and wistfully of Spain. They still dream of that nation across the Mediterranean as a special, lush paradise. Legend has it that when the last Moorish King of Granada, Boabdil, fled that splendid city he paused on a distant hilltop, looked back and wept. His mother regarded him with scorn and said, "Do not weep like a woman for something you could not hold as a man!"

Today's Moroccans do not weep as women over Spain—but sometimes they *do* sigh a little.

Chapter VIII

TEEN-AGE PROFILES: VEILED AND UNVEILED

It is eight-thirty in the morning on a bright fall day and the sprawling white city of Tangier glistens in the sun. At the dockside, long grey freighters rock gently in the Atlantic waters; off in the distance, the mountains are still purple-shadowed with morning dew; and in the sun-browned fields outside town, early farm workers are already hand-threshing or plowing with camel teams.

This is Tangier, queen city of Morocco, sitting on the far north point of Africa as it juts into the sea.

On a white balcony, six stories above the noisy street of *Musa ben Nusair,* Janine Morell sips hot breakfast chocolate and reviews her history lesson one last time. At fifteen and as a second-year student at École du Sacre Coeur, her lessons are difficult, her mood is serious. The sea breezes blow teasingly over her navy flannel school uniform and tug at the sleekly brushed hair, pulled back in a severe pony-tail. But there will be no time for the breezes till late afternoon.

"Today is an exam day," she explains, her schoolgirl English pleasantly accented. "I am high in my class but I must stay there if I am to qualify for the university in France."

Inside the six-room family apartment, Madame Morell is busy feeding a cageful of pastel parakeets and giving orders for the day to the Berber housemaid, a brown-skinned woman in the rough robes of the country. Bracelets jangle on her ankle as she pads barefoot over the tiled floor to the kitchen. Up from the street comes the shrill cry of Arab peddlers, hawking fresh fish and oven-fresh *croissants* to apartment housewives. Janine closes her book with a sigh. Time to start the day.

«««««««« »»»»»»»»

In another section of the city, the morning sun slants into a courtyard and warms the slim shoulders of fourteen-year-old Fatima Hantout as she waters the potted jasmine and geraniums climbing against the tiles. Her walled-in house sits on *Rue des Cretiens,* just above the Socco Chico in the old casbah. A dozen family rooms, ranging two stories high, surround this courtyard, which is open to the sky. Fatima, in her long, straight morning dress of light pink satin, makes a pretty picture against the shiny walls of orange and blue tiles. A half dozen younger brothers and sisters scramble and play about her feet. In the shadowy kitchen, separated from the courtyard by a beaded string curtain, Señora Hantout is chatting with the housemaids. Ahmed Ben Hantout, the father of the house, has already left for his tailoring shop and the home is filled with the pleasant hum and bustle of women's routines.

Fatima is shy but pleased to talk to you, using a hesitant Spanish rather than the Arabic which is her native tongue. If you, too, are female, she can face you without her customary face-veil, her olive-toned skin very young and free of make-up.

"This is just an ordinary day, please Allah," she says

softly. "We Arab girls lead a quiet life, but I will show you what I can." It is not until much later, until you are really friends, that Fatima can admit that this is, indeed, a very special day, a golden day.

Since most of Fatima's days—and life—were spent within the four walls of this house, her feet take her quickly over the pathway of her chores. Of course, there were no classes. Like most Moroccan city girls, Fatima has gone to school only until she was nine and could read and write a little Arabic. Her mother has trained her in keeping household accounts, however, so she is is quick with simple numbers.

"We have two housemaids," Fatima explains as we follow her up the steep tile stairs to the bedrooms, rimmed by an interior second-story balcony. "Almost every house has help, and our maids are blood-relatives of my father, poor farm girls who wanted to get out of the country."

Much of the time, young Fatima and the maids work as a team—the maids scrubbing and doing kitchen work while she goes from bedroom to bedroom, opening windows, folding off bed linen and smoothing out the bolsters and embroidered coverlets on the low divans. The dim rooms, lit only by the courtyard windows, smell cool and spicy. Before leaving each, Fatima sprinkles the floors with scented jasmine water, spreading the fragrant liquid with a dustcloth tied to her shoe. "We sleep in darkness and in perfume," she explains.

The question, "What do you do for fun—when the housework is over?" brings a look of startled surprise to Fatima's face. Was this not fun? Are we not pleased to be a guest in her home? Quickly the question is changed. "What do you like to do *best?*" we ask her. The surprise changes to a quick smile.

"This," she says proudly, and opens a heavy, carved chest. "This chest holds hours and hours of my life," she explains as she draws a half dozen cushions, heavily embroidered, and yards of cloth, also so intricately embroidered that it is as weighty as leather. "Since I have been a little girl I have embroidered most of the coverings in our salon, enough things for the bedrooms of my brothers and sisters—and this chest is full for the day of my own home. Arab girls are very quick and artistic with the needle."

Does she like to read? No, never. No novels, no newspapers? "No," she says simply, "I like to talk. I like to listen—and my mother and father tell me everything I need to know."

Does she like movies? we ask. But Fatima has never seen a movie. In Tangier, there are many cinemas. Most of the movies are in French or Spanish, but certain theaters show features made in Egypt or India, with Arabic soundtracks, usually intense, soap-opera love stories about hopeless romances. "Our life is different, I guess," Fatima tries to explain. "Movies are for men—or sometimes for housemaids—but no well-raised Moroccan girl would go to the movies—or anywhere except to visit friends and relatives. We are brought up quietly, as good daughters, so that we will be good wives." There is no TV in Morocco but radio is popular and, even as we talk, a high, skirling music is blaring up from the ground floor.

"Now," says Fatima firmly, "you must come with me for the big work of the day. I will go to the market for my mother. Tomorrow, two guests are coming for dinner, clothing merchants from the capital city of Rabat. Naturally, the womenfolk of the house will not eat with them, nor will we even be seen, since we are served second and apart. In the palaces of the pashas and the sultans, a true Moroccan feast or *diffa* may have twenty courses—but even in the house of Ahmed Ben Hantout we know how to prepare a feast!"

We are seated now in the main salon, right off the courtyard, while Fatima and her mother make out the market list. We can lounge comfortably on the long, fat bolsters used in Arab households instead of chairs and admire the group of camel-hide ottomans drawn around a heavy, short-legged brass tray. The walls are hung with alternate panels of heavy green, yellow and pink satin, with no other furniture or decorations in the room except a brass pot, sending up the blue, heavy smoke of burning incense.

Presently, a country cousin patters in and serves each of us a glass of mint tea, the national drink of Morocco, hot and heavily sweetened.

Fatima explains the shopping list. "We buy today and cook tomorrow," she says. Then she outlines the menu for the feast.

The Moslem Holy Book, the Koran, allows each man to have three wives, if he chooses and provided he treats them all with equality. In the Hantout household, there is obviously only one wife—and Señora Hantout looks almost as young as her daughter. In fact, married at thirteen, she is still in her twenties. Unlike her daughter, however, she wears heavy eye make-up, nail polish and high-heeled, Western-style pumps, as opposed to Fatima's soft yellow leather scuffs. Sitting together on the big lime-colored bolster, they look like a couple of tanned teen-agers, giggling and planning a party.

While her mother collects market baskets, Fatima hurries to her room to dress for the street. Moments later, she comes down wearing a full, ankle-length *djellaba* of light white serge, a head veil and a dainty, lace-trimmed hanky tied over her face, across the middle of the nose. Nothing remains of the Fatima of a moment ago except the expressive eyes and a glimpse of forehead. "I am ready," she says as we two step from the cool courtyard into the hot, cobblestoned street.

Instantly, we are caught in a whirl of noise and color. The huge market, just a few blocks away, in the center of the casbah, is open to the sky, with stall after stall of garden produce and other merchandise. Fatima stops first at a spice booth, pointing with authority to this or that pile of spice heaped on a straw mat. A little saffron, some paprika, a cup of cinnamon—each is wrapped separately in a twist of brown paper. Last of all we buy half a dozen live pigeons, tied at the feet. The shopping takes two hours, while Fatima, in true Moroccan housewife style, haggles and bargains over every purchase.

Could we stop at one of the sidewalk cafes for a rest and another mint tea? Never, explains Fatima firmly. Such public behavior is only for men. "But," she says cheerfully, "we will get a chance to go out on the street again when I bring my father his lunch!"

«««««««« »»»»»»»»

The Hantout tailoring shop is a one-room factory on the second floor of the municipal donkey stable, right off the main market place. The only light comes in the open doorway and from a single bulb dangling from the ceiling. In the shadows, one can see two large looms, strung with the coarse brown and white wool so favored for men's *djellabas* or robes. Four young boys, tailors' apprentices, squat nearby, winding wool for the looms or snipping basting threads from half-finished garments. In the center of the floor, Fatima's father sits sprawled-legged, turning the wheel of a sewing machine with his bare foot as he busies both hands with the heavy cloth. In the corner, a radio blares.

The entire second floor of the building is made up of small workshops, opening out to a balcony over an open-air courtyard. Below, several hundred donkeys bray and pull at their tethers. It costs just two cents a day for farmers to stable their beasts here, including water and an armload of hay.

Father Hantout stands to greet us, full of grace and dignity. He wears a coarse, workday cotton *djellaba,* but his head is twisted with a fresh white turban. His heavily-bearded face is kind as he takes the covered lunch pan from his daughter. An apprentice scuttles on all fours to remove the saucepan of mint tea, simmering over a small charcoal brazier. The lunch is put on to heat. Both older weavers nod a greeting to Fatima; the younger boys say nothing. A Moroccan girl may wander unmolested—and often ungreeted—through the city streets. A man is as respectful outside the home as he is within.

On the stairway leading down, we pass a blind beggar huddled in a corner, his hand outstretched for alms. Fatima fumbles in her pocket for a few coins. "Give to the poor" is also a teaching of the Koran and the beggar's singsong "Blessings in the name of Allah!" echoes after us as we clatter down the rude stairs to the street.

«««««««« »»»»»»»»

All through the later afternoon, Fatima and I sit around the courtyard fountain while she darts her needle in and out of an embroidery frame. She chats quietly, with a feeling of time and leisure. Occasionally, she pauses to hum a lullaby to her infant sister, dozing on a cushion beside her. The baby soon snuggles back to sleep and Fatima smiles like a contented little mother. Suddenly her voice goes soft, her face solemn. The embroidery work lies idle in her hands.

"I am pleased to have you with me as a friend on this special day," she says with elaborate Arab courtesy.

Curious, we ask what she means, and our Moroccan friend's

face flushes with a shy happiness. "Today is *not* just an ordinary day," she admits. "It is a day of special joy. . . . Last night the first bolts of silk, our traditional engagement gift, arrived from my bridegroom. I will be married before the end of the year."

Fatima's story is like that of thousands of other Moroccan girls who follow the age-old marriage customs. All is arranged; almost final. And yet, according to strict custom, neither young person has met face to face in their "grown-up" years.

And is she happy about this wedding? Will she really be pleased, we ask, with a husband she has never seen?

Fatima smiles quickly, a grown-up smile, as if to say she is sorry if we cannot understand, and answers, "Of course. My parents are wise. Allah is wise. I would be a very unwise girl not to make my life a happy one."

«««««««« »»»»»»»»

At four o'clock the next afternoon, I stretch out beside Janine Morell on the warm beach, admiring her red swim suit, bright against the sand.

"This is the best hour of the day," she says. "Lessons are over and I still have a few hours before dinner and the evening study. Father never gets home from the sugar factory —he has been a manager there for years—until about seven o'clock. I still have part of my day ahead." Janine's English is excellent, with a full vocabulary she has been acquiring since fourth grade.

"Do you come to the beach every day?" we ask.

"In the summer and on these last sunny days, yes," she explains. "It is never really cold here, not snow-cold. But in late fall and spring, my friends and I usually play at some sport at school or go bicycling in the country. Then, when the winter rains come, we visit at home. Each of us has her records —Louis Armstrong, Yves Montand—and even your Elvis Presley."

And movies? "Oh, yes," she answers with a laugh. "I am like any teen-ager. I dream my dreams in the cinema. All the best French films come here, and many English ones, too. I see them mostly with Mama, who is passionate for the movies. And we have music—concerts during the winter. And we have all the books we want, French papers every day and all the French magazines—*Jour de France, Paris Match*—everything. We are just like Paris in our lives—except that we are in Africa and Paris is miles away." We sit silently as a small, barefoot Arab approaches, carrying a big straw tray of peanuts. Janine searches her beach bag for some francs and buys a handful of nuts from the boy, murmuring a few words of thanks in Arabic.

"And you also speak Arabic?" we ask in awe.

"No, no," she says. "Not really. But I was born in Tangier, have spent my life here. And everyone must know several languages. You will notice that even the street signs are in three languages—French, Spanish and Arabic. We all live together—no, we live more side by side. But we respect each other's customs and we must talk to each other."

Do you have Arab friends? "Not now," she answers sadly. "When I was younger, we had a house outside town, near the beach. Then I played with Arab children, mostly the little girls and boys shepherding the sheep. It was all easy and natural because little children are *all* alike. Now my friends are mostly my school chums . . . French-Moroccans like my-self."

"We French have become fewer and fewer in Morocco since

the days of their freedom," Janine explains. "Many Frenchmen have gone back to France—but even today I have one grandmother in Paris and one in Marrakesh, in central Morocco."

And about boys and dating? "Yes," she explains, "all my friends and I, too, are interested in boys—but we are too serious as students to give them much time. At the holidays, we might have little parties in our homes, but mostly with brothers and cousins mixed in. We all must study hard so we can qualify for the universities in France. Already, my older sister is there to study agriculture. Her fiance manages a large melon farm in the *bled,* or countryside, and she wishes to work with him."

"I want to major in the arts," she says. And then, more hesitantly, she continues, "Some day I will be a dress designer. I made this—" she points to her beige linen beach bag, embroidered with vivid shell designs. "And I have made many of my summer things. I never bother with winter." She laughs. "Then it is just school—and my old blue uniform!"

Later, as the sun turns red over the water, Janine and I pack the beach things and walk up the crowded city streets to her home. Center city is as busy as New York, with white-gloved policemen in the bustle of traffic. The sidewalk cafes are already crowded with French couples, enjoying an aperitif and looking out at the colorful Tangier parade of Arabs in flowing robes, women, veiled and Berber, and the constant stream of donkeys moving patiently out of town and toward the hills.

The Morell apartment is warm with activity and noise. From the kitchen comes the light clatter of dishes as the Berber maid prepares the evening meal. Janine puts on her favorite Louis Armstrong LP for us and we hear Madame Morell in the next room, chattering on the telephone in rapid French. Promptly at seven, Monsieur Morell arrives home, a slim, mustached man in a grey flannel suit.

At suppertime, we sit about the round table, circled in by the light of a modern hanging glass globe. The maid shuffles about in the surrounding dimness, serving us hot consomme, then liver paté, with cheese and salad and a platter of tiny fruit tarts. The conversation is in French, then in English; talk is of books, the weather, school—easy, at-home topics. I feel familiar here, almost as though I had left Morocco behind.

Suddenly, Janine jumps up from the table, saying, "Excuse me, please!" Then, "I want *you* to see something!"

Together we go to the open balcony. In the last light of day, we can look down over the city to the balcony of a Moslem minaret, a short distance away. Here a *muezzin,* the prayer caller, stands erect, wailing out over the city to summon all faithful Moslems to kneel in the last prayer of the day. As the faint tone of his singsong cry dies out, we see his dim white form bend in reverence, his head touching the ground in rhythmic prayer. In silence, we watch this impressive, age-old scene. And then, for us, Janine and me—and for our Moroccan friends in bright apartments or high-walled houses—the same night falls over Tangier.

Chapter IX

DUST ON THE PEARLS

JUST FOR ONE chapter, I'd like to put aside the pad, pencil and black and white statistics of a reporter. Just for one chapter, I'd prefer to change places with a storyteller in a *souk,* holding attention with once-upon-a-times and make-believe.

The story I want to tell is not a fantasy "out of the *Arabian Nights,*" though it does have veiled women, mystery and romance. Rather, it is an idea that occurred on a quiet, sunny Moroccan afternoon. I was visiting an old friend stationed at the U.S. Air Base at Nouasseur, outside Casablanca, when a little Moroccan housemaid slipped in to serve a tray of iced soft drinks and potato chips.

My friend told me all she knew about this girl and her recent, mysterious behavior. Not all the facts were there; just enough intriguing and unanswered questions to suggest a story. So this is the half-true tale of young Fatima of Casablanca. This is what happened. Or, at least, I think this is what happened. . . .

«««««««« »»»»»»»»

"John," Major Chapman's wife said to him at breakfast, "I have had the oddest feeling for days that Fatima is trying to tell me something."

"Then why doesn't she speak up?" he asked cheerfully, pouring himself a third cup of coffee.

"Don't be silly," his wife said. "You know she doesn't speak English. And I know so little French . . . and not even enough Arabic to bless her if she sneezes."

"Then how do you know she's trying to tell you something?" he asked.

"Well, she just sort of *aches* toward me lately. I catch her staring at me when she should be working. And each night, when it's time for her to run for the bus, she stands by the front door. . . . There's just a look on her face that makes me know she wants to say something to me."

The bright, warm sun of a Moroccan fall slanted through the windows into the little dining room and fell across the remains of a ham-and-eggs breakfast, the morning mail with the U.S. postmarks and a slim copy of the Paris edition of the Herald Tribune, flown down to the air base during each night. The furniture was American, the look of the house was American, the people and even the smell of Major Chapman's cigarette was American, but outside the sky was an unclouded African blue and even the air glowed bright, as if reflecting the surrounding miles of sandy plain. Major Chapman leaned back in his chair and smiled fondly at his wife.

"I never saw Fatima's face," he said, "so I don't get the message."

Mrs. Chapman shrugged impatiently. "She doesn't wear her face veil when we two are alone in the house. Incidentally, she's very, very pretty. Shy and so young but very delicate and sweet. And she has a little pattern of blue-dot tribal markings tattooed on her chin. Her mother was part of a mountain tribe before she married and moved into Casablanca. And since Fatima is the oldest child, she got handed a little family pride, I guess. There are eight other children in that family, you know. . . ."

"I thought you couldn't talk to her," her husband teased.

"Oh, we *talk*. After all, Fatima's worked for us for three years and I see her day in and day out. I can say her word for 'hello' and she can say my word for 'scrub brush' and we point and count on our fingers. But we don't *really* talk."

"You'd think, if she had any brains, she'd pick up a little English," her husband said abruptly.

"She's *very* bright," his wife said defensively. "You think because she doesn't like to use the dishwasher and the electric mixer and such things that she's backward. That's not true at all. In fact, she can clean better than I can. She is very, very clean. And so quick and so honest. And, after all, John, the child is only fourteen years old."

At that moment, young John put his head out from under the tablecloth where he was having a comfortable few moments of play before school. "Mother," he said firmly, "I need a whole new set of soldiers."

"I thought your grandmother sent you a big boxful from the States for your birthday not six months ago."

"She did. But that was six months ago. They are all *friendly* soldiers now. I need some new *enemies*." And he ducked back under the tablecloth.

Occasionally, a jet plane cut high across the sky with a fading mechanical scream, setting a vibration through the windowpanes of the little frame house. Major Chapman took a small notebook from the pocket of his uniform jacket and began checking down a list of names and notations.

"One thing I do know about Fatima, John," his wife said. "Even if I don't understand what she's been trying to tell me lately—she thinks *you're* funny."

He looked up in surprise. *"Funny!"* he exclaimed. "Why, I hardly do more than nod to her. And I certainly don't boff around the house like a Hollywood comic. . . ."

"I know. But she just thinks you're funny. You amuse her somehow. Many times, when you burst in the door or go dashing out somewhere, she turns and smiles at me and her eyes are just shooting with laughter. I mean, she *likes* you 'funny,' " his wife amended.

"O.K.," Major Chapman said, "tell your little Arab comedienne that the yakkiest major in the United States Air Force is taking a group of those crazy jets up to the Rota base and won't be back for two days. I'll bet she splits her veil laughing." He stood to button his jacket.

His wife leaned over to be kissed good-by and felt the small nag of both worry and pride she had felt ever since the first days they had been married and the first days she had watched him fly away. "We'll miss you," she said softly. "Don't take any wooden *pesetas*."

«««««««« »»»»»»»»

At ten o'clock sharp, an old, rickety bus stopped just outside the guarded gates of the air base and disgorged an oversized load. Here were the mechanics' assistants, the janitors and the construction workers who were employed around the great hangars and runways, the base country club and the service areas—the unskilled Moroccan personnel who helped man the huge air base. And here were the white-draped and veiled "Fatimas," some fat and waddling in their robes, some slim and quick as children, who served as household help in the officers' homes. Some were rightfully called Fatima and some were not. But Fatima is a proud and sacred name—that of the daughter of the great Prophet Mohammed

—and any Moroccan woman was proud to answer to it. So the foreigners, with a great turnover in help and confused sometimes by those look-alike bodies, swathed like bandaged thumbs, called all their maids Fatima.

The Chapmans' Fatima got off the bus last, bunching up her long skirts with one hand and clutching a bottle of jasmine water in the other. Her soft yellow-leather scuffs made a light *slip-slip* sound as she padded down the neat residential streets. It was a part of the day she loved, the time of coming to work. The trim rows of houses, mostly five-room affairs in white clapboard, stood in precise economy on narrow streets. Here there were some trees, strips of clipped lawn and flowers planted around the doorways. She loved the look of the cars standing at the curbs, glinting in the sun. And she loved the scatter of tricycles on the lawns and the little preschool children in cowboy overalls and plaid shirts, beginning the day with a shout and a clatter of toy wagons. Even though, in the Moslem faith, a dog is considered an unclean beast and not to be touched, Fatima felt a small pride at each neighborhood animal that wagged its tail and snuffled at the hem of her robes. There was the Chapmans' big spaniel, and the next-door Irish setter and two boxers from down the block—big, strange-appearing dogs that ate as much as men. She loved their look and sound. It was all part of the marvel of coming to work. And even after three years, Fatima was awed that she could be there at all.

Clearly she remembered the first day. It had been at the time when they had known for sure that her brother Ahmed was dying. He was one year younger than Fatima, a brown-skinned, wiry boy, with dark, liquid eyes and a quick, rapid energy. Fatima had been nicknamed "little mother" because almost from babyhood it was she who took care of him. When he was just four, she walked him to his first classes at the Koran school, pulling his hand from hers and making him promise to be good when she left him at the door of the tiny, windowless classroom. Even when he was old enough to go to school by himself, she picked him up at noontime, dressing carefully in her long, pink-satin street dress, savoring the spicy smells of the casbah and the warm, worn smoothness of cobblestones under her bare feet.

At nine years old, Ahmed was finished with religious school. Having mastered the long, singsong phrases of the Koran, he was ready for his first job as a tailor's apprentice. Then he spent a ten-hour day in a tailor's booth, in the heart of the casbah, sitting cross-legged on a stone floor to pull basting threads, or running errands for the master. Fatima had turned ten and was veiled to the world, but Ahmed kept her filled with stories of the men at work and the gossip of the casbah. There were five other children by then, though Allah had seen fit to bless the family with only one male child, Ahmed. And with five new mouths to feed, Fatima's mother went to work for the Chapmans and "little mother" watched at home.

Ahmed's first coughs came in the cold, persistent rain of winter and Fatima's mother tried to coax him to health with hot mint tea, the steam sweet with sugar, and a bit of folded blanket to sit on when he worked. But when the bright brown eyes glazed with fever and the thin body humped with coughing, a physician was called. The doctor had only to put into words what they had feared. It was tuberculosis.

Near the end of the last weeks, Fatima thought she herself would waste away with terror and loneliness. Without Ahmed, the house would be like a place of the dead. The little children did not seem to know—but the parents knew and Fatima knew. And near the end, Ahmed knew, too, because his mother allowed him to rest on the best bolsters, covering him with embroidered spreads she had made and saved from her girlhood. And harking back to the superstitions she believed she had left with her tribe in the mountains, she shaved his head, leaving little tufts of "good luck" hair standing stiff on his fevered skull.

It was then that Fatima simply changed places with her mother, full of fear at leaving the casbah for the first time, and went to work for the Chapmans. Fatima could still remember the kind but puzzled look on Mrs. Chapman's face when she knocked on the front door. And three weeks later Ahmed was dead, bound tight and thin in white winding sheets and laid out on a wooden litter. Fatima got home from the Chapmans in time for the pre-sundown burial.

So it had all become bound together—the Chapmans, death, life and Fatima's growing up.

«««««««« »»»»»»»»

By noontime, the house was neat and quiet. It was too small a place for a maid really, a pre-fab house like all the others, square-roomed and precise. The kitchen hummed with electrical equipment and the living room and bedrooms were anonymous with modern, foam-rubbered furniture and draperies and coverings of bright plaid and muted prints. It was the kind of house that could be lived in with comfort and left without regrets when one was transferred to another army post. But to Fatima is was as lavish as a pasha's palace.

Each morning she carefully folded off her outer robes and —if the Major was away—her face veil, placing the little heap on the floor of the hall closet. Then she slipped off her shoes. In the beginning, Mrs. Chapman had tried to make signals about keeping on the shoes but Fatima knew it was easier to work and serve in the sure-footed silence of bare feet. Also, she was too proud to try to explain the economies of going barefoot. But she was always careful to arrive well-scrubbed, her feet and the palms of her hands rubbed attractively with the red-brown dust of henna.

The days had a peaceful sameness. In the kitchen, the radio played softly. Mrs. Chapman wrote letters, tidied drawers, did the laundry in the great humming machine which Fatima never dared to touch or sat in the little living room leafing through magazines.

Fatima dusted, ironed, swept and scrubbed, doing the entire house from one room to the other every day. She loved sitting on the cool white tiles of the bathroom floor, polishing at the shiny legs of the fixtures and, when all was clean, she dampened cloths with jasmine water and tied them to her bare feet, skating over the tile and the linoleum in the kitchen and Johnnie's bedroom till the house had the delicate, fragrant scent of a harem. Mrs. Chapman often smiled and shook her head fondly as she watched the daily ritual. Sometimes Fatima found herself waiting until she was sure Mrs. Chapman would see, because she knew it amused her.

Mrs. Chapman always made lunch, setting Fatima's share neatly on a napkin at the kitchen table. Even when she herself drank only a cup of coffee, Fatima was served a full meal of left-overs—thick soups or a dish of hot dogs with milk and cookies. In the beginning there had been too much food and Fatima sensed that Mrs. Chapman wanted her to wrap it up, to take it home. But she ate only what she required. She was *paid* for her work. Yet in three years Fatima had rarely needed to eat in her own home, her share going to her little sisters. Thus the matter had been settled with pride—but without words on either side.

It was almost like being in the house with a sister, Fatima felt, except this older sister seemed so much younger with so little work to do, no sickness, nothing to worry about and only one small male child to look after. So Fatima worried for her sometimes, sighing with relief when big Major Chapman came home at night, safe again and so welcomed that it made her smile.

Today the mood of the house was subdued. Mrs. Chapman was busy making phone calls about a benefit dance at the Officers' Club, talking rapidly in her strange language, chain smoking. Fatima was careful to walk quietly and not to sing as she worked, yet she was disappointed. Today, she had hoped desperately, would have been the right day to try to explain. It had to happen so soon. She couldn't keep her excitement, her worry cooped up much longer. And yet it was all so hard to say without words. At one o'clock, Mrs. Chapman dashed out to a bridge luncheon and Fatima was alone in the sunny silence of the house.

«««««««« »»»»»»»»

That night of all nights, Mrs. Chapman wished her husband had been home, instead of far off at the Rota air base. It was just a small thing that had happened but it troubled her. The bridge luncheon had been pleasant and, except for the bother of a new arrangement—a grab-bag booth—the plans for the benefit dance were going well, as did all social activities in this military oasis. But something was wrong.

After dinner, young John lay on the floor, puzzling over third-grade homework and groaning with mock despair. His mother stared down at his soft brown hair, the pencil clutched in stubby fingers.

"Johnnie," she asked brightly, "were you by any chance playing with my jewelry today?"

"What do you think I am?" he demanded brusquely. "Some silly girl?"

She sighed. In her heart she knew it hadn't been Johnnie. But at five o'clock she had come into the quiet house and changed into a sweater and skirt, putting her earrings and wrist watch into the top drawer of her dressing table. The drawer had had a different look, neat but changed, a change as slight as a breeze passing over grass or flowers rearranged in a vase. But changed.

Quickly, almost unwillingly, Mrs. Chapman had checked over the jewelry, a collection of inexpensive costume items, a formal wrist watch and a few antique pieces belonging to Major Chapman's mother. Then she checked the other drawers—the handbags, the white gloves, the nylon hose in flowered plastic envelopes. Everything was in perfect order. It was just the jewelry drawer that had been touched, carefully and surreptitiously, by someone who hadn't wanted it noticed. But one five-strand choker showed clearly the reddish touches of powdered henna. Fatima had been wearing her pearls.

«««««««««« »»»»»»»»»»

Outside the big PX shopping center at the air base, Fatima pulled the end of her white robe across her veiled face, staring demurely and impersonally at the ground as a group of airmen walked by.

"I'll be just a minute," Mrs. Chapman had said. "I've got everything we need except salad things and some of the raisin cereal for Johnnie."

As a non-American, Fatima and the other servants on the

base were not allowed inside the Post Exchange, a shopping center combination of grocery, drugstore and dry goods. But she loved these visits—the brief ride in the car, the shiny windows crowded with American products and the companionship of helping Mrs. Chapman load the big brown paper bags in the back seat. And at the house, Fatima sorted the groceries, putting the fresh things in the refrigerator and lining the pantry shelves precisely with canned goods, matching them carefully by the pictures on the labels. In her own home, there was never this plentitude—just a bit of shopping done day by day. A chicken for ten people or some fish with rice, perhaps. Her family ate to live, counting each day and each meal as a gift from Allah; there was none of this joy, this playing with food and plenty.

Fatima wandered over to look through the big glass panes of the PX, watching Mrs. Chapman as she picked a shopping cart and disappeared into the crowd. There was music inside, a look of color and movement. . . . Then, suddenly, Fatima felt her young breath come short, an almost choking feeling around her heart. In one corner of a display window lay a heap of jewels, falling, tumbling and twisting in beady brilliance. Behind them was a sign which meant nothing to Fatima: "FALL CLEARANCE: POP-IT BEADS AT HALF PRICE. WHILE THEY LAST!"

This collection of summer jewelry—red, sea-green, blue, bright yellow and synthetic pearl beads—seemed to move and multiply before her eyes until they were almost alive in their splendor. So many, so many. . . . She leaned against the glass, her hot palms pressed tight against the cool pane. It was almost too much for the eye to absorb, such color, such wealth. There was enough here for a queen, for a harem. Enough for a bride. . . .

"Fatima, Fatima," Mrs. Chapman was saying behind her, almost irritably. "Please. I bought more than I expected and these bags are heavy. I can't get out the keys to the car." Fatima snapped from her reverie and hurried to carry the bags. The color of the beads was still before her eyes, refusing to let her see clearly.

I am too proud to ask, Fatima thought to herself, holding her lower lip in white teeth to stop its trembling. If I asked, she would get them for me. But it must be a gift. At this time of life, it must be a gift. I must not bring bad luck. I must stay too proud to ask.

«««««««« »»»»»»»»

Never had the bus ride back to Casablanca seemed so long. On most evenings, Fatima stared out the window for the whole fifteen-mile run, savoring the familar sights of the farm villages, with the mud huts crown-topped with straw and the black and white storks flitting over refuse heaps. The camel teams, plodding around water wheels or treading out the grain for threshing, were as familiar as family pets, their lumpy silhouettes showing dark against the sunset sky. Along the edges of the road, Arab farmers rode their donkeys sidesaddle, carrying loads of melons and charcoal off to the mountain villages. It was a going-home time of night, usually filled with contentment and a conviction that Allah was good. Now Fatima could see nothing but the windowful of beads, bright, graceful, wanting to be touched. And time was growing so short. That was what she needed to explain to Mrs. Chapman. In two weeks it would all be over . . . and it would just be begun.

The plans were final, his gifts had been sent—and in two weeks she would go to him. Fatima had not seen her bridegroom since she was a young child, but already she loved him. She was ready for love.

Negotiations had been made between the parents of the two families; everything would be done according to Moslem custom. Her bridegroom, just turned seventeen, was the son of the tailor for whom young Ahmed had worked. He knew Fatima came without a dowry. His family was not wealthy either but his gifts had been proper, even lavish—several bolts of middle-grade blue and green silk and six flacons of perfume. Fatima's mother had worked for weeks over a wedding gown with head and face veilings of the same silk.

Fatima sighed as she swayed with the rhythm of the bus. She did not mind about the dowry; she knew that eight children were more valuable than a purseful of francs. But she wanted so much to come to her husband full of love *and* beauty. On that wedding night, when she was taken to his home for the first time, to enter those high white walls and his room as his wife, she wanted him to look on beauty. She stared down now at her small brown hands and let them flutter out on her lap until the wrists were bare. She had the silks, the perfumes and the love—but there should be something of her own to show willingness to please. Her wrists, her neck, her slim brown ankles should be covered with jewels.

Later that night, Fatima lay on her bolsters, careful not to move lest she wake her two little sisters at her side. But sleep came slowly. She knew she had been dreaming when she woke up feeling the beads in her hands, cool and round to the touch.

At the air base, Major Chapman mixed himself a pre-bed scotch and soda and said, "I wouldn't worry about her handling your things, honey. I know how fond you are of her, but, after all, Fatima's just a kid. Kids like to play with things. If you had a drawerful of dolls, she'd probably be playing with them. It's not important enough to worry about."

«««««««« »»»»»»»»

In the next two weeks, time ticked by on a slow clock. Padding about the Chapman house, Fatima prayed and prayed to Allah and, in her fervor, she often included Mrs. Chapman in her prayers, joining her goodness and abundance with the fabled benevolence of Allah. Mrs. Chapman had always understood before, she had always been kind. Even in her silence, she had understood the pain of Ahmed's going. She had understood about food at lunchtime, a hot cup of tea on a bitter winter morning or an umbrella at five o'clock for a chill, fall drizzle. And she had understood about pride. She would certainly understand about love, Fatima knew, but love was something you couldn't point to, nor draw its shape with your hands nor count it on your fingers.

On each shopping day, outside the PX, Fatima watched with a dry fear as the heap of cut-rate beads got lower and lower. Already, most of the reds and sea-greens were gone. And then one afternoon, her heart beat with joy as she saw Mrs. Chapman pause beside the beads, hold a couple of strands to her neckline and then gather the entire heap into her shopping cart. The prayer "Allah is good, Allah is great!" sang through Fatima's head until she felt it might burst with praise and thanks. The girl was convinced that by the magic of love, Mrs. Chapman had understood her need, had heard her prayers. Her mistress had bought for Fatima the gift of wedding beads.

At the cashier's counter, Mrs. Chapman said, "I'm taking

all that's left of these pop-it beads. We're making up a grab-bag booth for the dance on Saturday and they will make nice little packages. . . ."

«««««««« »»»»»»»»

At five that afternoon, just before bus time, Fatima toured the little house, padding from room to room, looking with tear-soft eyes at every chair, every ashtray, every picture on the walls. In his bedroom, she stooped over Johnnie, gently touching his hair as he played with his toys. She wanted to remember this house and these people forever—and this was the last time.

In the kitchen, the shopping had been put neatly on the shelves, the paper sacks burned in the outdoor trash can. Fatima traced her fingertips over the cool surface of the refrigerator, checked the low flame burning under a pot roast on the stove. She shut her eyes once, to make sure the picture was printed forever on her memory. Only then did she allow herself to scoop up the strings of beads in her hands.

Quietly, on her little hennaed feet, she slipped into the living room, where Mrs. Chapman stood looking out at the street. In a torrent of singsong Arabic, Fatima poured out her thanks, holding the beads at her neck, at her wrists, explaining about the wedding and the new life, with excitement lighting her dark eyes till they shone.

"Take them, dear, take them," Mrs. Chapman said, gesturing with both hands. "Take them—they are nothing at all. It was just that silly grab-bag thing and. . . ." She believes I bought them for *her,* Mrs. Chapman realized suddenly. Fatima believes those beads are my gift to her. The girl darted forward and kissed her mistress on both cheeks.

Mrs. Chapman was conscious of her warmth, the tremble

of her body and the clinging scent of jasmine. "I mean, dear, that I *do* want you to have those beads." She was surprised to feel tears in her own eyes.

«««««««« »»»»»»»»

"Well, we'll be off to Rota again tomorrow," Major Chapman said to his wife and then, "Johnnie, if you're going to play with that truck, take it to your own room. I want a few minutes of quiet with your mother before dinner."

Mrs. Chapman sat silently for a moment. "Fatima hasn't come in for the past three days," she said thoughtfully.

"Maybe she's ill," her husband said.

"No, she hasn't missed a day in three years. I just know she's never coming back."

Her husband shrugged. "If she wanted to quit, you'd have thought she'd say something. We didn't pay her much but you were certainly nice to her. She could have said *something*. They're funny people, these Arabs."

Mrs. Chapman stood and walked behind her husband's chair. Leaning over, she kissed him on the cheek. Then she gently rubbed her hand over the soft bristle of his crewcut hair. "*You* don't understand, John," she said softly. "I understand *at last* what she was saying. Her excitement, her joy over those beads . . . when I remember the look on her face when she thanked me, I understand everything. And she trusted me to understand. I guess all women use the same language when they talk about love."

Chapter X

A FINAL WORD

U*ntil you make the journey to Morocco in person . . .* there is a custom in this country, based on one of Mohammed's teachings, that the traveler or wayfarer, weary from his journeys, must be given shelter, food and hospitality for a period of three days. This, in a land where the sun is bright, mountains are steep and roads are rough, assures the stranger of a respite in his journeying.

In this book, I have thought of you readers as potential travelers in Morocco. I hope you have experienced in these pages the warmth, welcome (and information) which Mohammed says is your due.

Index

Maureen Daly

was born in County Tyrone, Northern Ireland, and grew up in Fond du Lac, Wisconsin. She first won literary distinction when she was sixteen, with a short story called *Sixteen* which placed first in a national short story contest sponsored by *Scholastic Magazine* and was selected for the annual O. Henry Memorial Award volume. Her first novel, *Seventeenth Summer,* won the Dodd, Mead Intercollegiate Literary Fellowship contest and quickly became a best seller. She has never stopped writing since—writing vigorously, simply and always with a new appeal.

Her articles and short stories have appeared in many national magazines and, as a reporter-columnist for the *Chicago Tribune* and later as an Associate Editor of *Ladies' Home Journal,* Miss Daly toured throughout the entire United States, as well as foreign countries from Iceland to Italy to Nigeria, talking with and writing about people, their interests and their problems.

On each trip abroad, Miss Daly found time to visit Spain, touring from the Pyrenees to the southern Mediterranean, and finally established a second home there, outside of Malaga. With her husband, writer William McGivern, and two children, Megan and Patrick, Miss Daly now spends a part of each year in southern Spain.

Renewals:

(800) 471-0991
www.santaclaracountylib.org